Mercy Jeyaraja Rao

Mercy Jeyaraja Rao

My Story

Numbers 6:24-26
Bible

© 2021

Published in the United States by Nurturing Faith, Macon, GA.

Nurturing Faith is a book imprint of Good Faith Media (goodfaithmedia.org).

Library of Congress Cataloging-in-Publication Data is available.

ISBN: 978-1-63528-136-1

Acknowledgments

My loving gratitude to the following:

Sandy Wisener, whose constant encouragement helped me write my story.

My dear friend Carol Cantrell, who introduced me to Ingeborg Walther, Professor of Practice Emerita of Germanic Language and Literature, Duke University, who read the draft and corrected and edited the manuscript.

Robert Money, Sydnor Money, and Don Rairdon for their constant encouragement and labor of love in getting the manuscript ready for publication.

Family and friends for their prayers which have upheld me.

To God, who gave me a story of his redemption and release.

Contents

Preface

Do not doubt God, who made you who you are. Do not compare yourself to anyone, and do not covet another's gifts. Stir up the gifts God has given to you. You are unique and special.

Why am I writing *My Story*? Over the years the women around the world who have blessed my life, my former students and friends, have been asking me who I really am. I did not feel worthy. I am who I am because of God's grace. Someone defined grace as "getting what you don't deserve. Mercy is not getting what you deserve." I have prayed and sought God's will, and from his Word he confirmed. So here I go with it: "Things we have heard and known, things our ancestors have told us. We will not hide them from their descendants; we will tell the next generation the praiseworthy deeds of the LORD, his power, and the wonders he has done" (Ps 78:3–4).

The story of my life is not about my accomplishments. The choice I made in the year 1947, when I turned my life over to Jesus, has made all the difference. A man of God prayed, "Lord, get me out of the way and let the instrument be forgotten and you get all the glory." This is my prayer as I write my story.

In 2008 while I was walking on the beaches of Charleston, South Carolina, I picked up a seashell, and these words came to me:

The Sea Shell

Lonely and tossed by an angry ocean it lay on the shore.
I held it and admired its beauty and perfect design.
My heart ached. Why is it alone? Does no one care?
I paused and questioned but got no answer.
Then, I heard a Voice.
It was the familiar voice. The Voice I heard over the years.
This is not you, my child. You are in the palm of my hand,
You are never alone.
The storms of life cannot destroy you.
I am your redeemer.
My love covers you. My Presence shelters you.
"Lord, do you love me so?" I asked.
I've doubted and questioned you. I have failed you.

Look at the broken pieces of my life.
All was silent…I waited…gently He whispered,
"I see you through My Son, Jesus,
In Him you are whole."
I wept…I knelt…I exclaimed,
"Thanks to Calvary's Cross…Thanks to the Empty Tomb…
What a Great Savior is mine!"

My life is a testament to God's love and my parents' love and acceptance. I know that Dad and Mom had their dreams for me, but they slipped aside and allowed me to pursue God's dream to be who I am. I wish I could see my mom and dad just once to say, "Thank you for letting me be who I am." Dad, I saw you and Mom sit in the front row at the opening of the new school building in Waltair Uplands. As Mr. PVG Raju, finance minister, AP, declared it open, I stood up and said, "The dream has come true," and saw big tears roll down your face. You let me be single and pursue a career. You helped me choose the direction of my life so I would reach the right destination. You prayed for me fervently. Many things remind me of you both. I love you. I miss you and look forward to being with you in the home above in the presence of Jesus. Until then, I will continue to see your smiling faces and feel your prayers covering me.

My life is a testament to God's grace and mercy that have kept me through sorrow, joy, and pain. The last day of every year, I seek a promise from God, and one year his promise was this: The God of the hitherto is yours in the hereafter; raise your Ebenezer. At the beginning of the year, there is a sense of uncertainty as to what lies in store for us. Yes, we have not been "this way before," but God is the constant friend. He never will leave nor forsake us. The hymn writer of "Abide with Me" says, "Change and decay in all around I see. Oh, Thou who changes not, abide with me." His presence in us gives us an inner peace and beauty. Let us radiate it and cultivate it with prayer and the study of God's Word.

When God speaks
Listen and obey.
When God opens a door
Enter—God holds the future.

Part One

My Life

Roots

Havajee Daniel and Mary Jeyaraja Rao

My father, Havajee Daniel Jeyaraja Rao, son of Havajee Seshagiri Rao, was born July 27, 1894, and died April 13, 1967. He used to say that one's background does not matter; it is who we are that matters. According to my father's brother, their father had been born into a family of priests, and my grandfather had been favored to become a priest to the king of Tanjore. It was only after my father passed away that I learned this, whereupon I asked my uncle to write an outline of the family history. Three days later, he gave me a handwritten history of his family and proudly said, "This is who we are and our heritage!" My father would have been mortified by such pride. One can be proud, humbled, or mortified by one's family background, but we are who we are, at least in part, because of those who have gone before us.

From my uncle I learned more about my paternal grandfather. When he was five years old, he went downtown with his mother. When the carriage stopped, a boy who looked like him and of the same age asked him for the candy he was eating. He gave him a little and was about to eat what was left when his mother requested to be driven back home. When he got home, he got a thorough scrubbing in the river, and his mother thrashed him. When he later asked her the reason for the confusion, she explained that he had been chosen by God to propitiate for the "untouchable," and in touching the boy he had defiled himself. This made no sense to him, and he began the search for a god who loves and accepts everyone.

"Does your God love everyone?" was the question he asked until he read the Bible and found the answer in John 3:16: "God so loved the world that he gave his one and only Son, that whoever believes in him shall not perish but have eternal life."

The only source of information I have about my father's family is the outline written by my uncle, Havajee Atreya Rao. My hope is that someone who reads my uncle's narrative will shed more light on this history (see Appendix). Dad's father passed away when I turned one year old. The last thing he did was feed me my first solid meal, a significant celebration with family and friends. The meal is rice and lentil, cooked soft, and ghee (clarified butter), served in a new silver bowl with a plate and a spoon. The grandfather or the oldest member of the family prays a blessing on the child and feeds the first spoonful of the meal.

A couple of years before his death, Grandfather came to live with my parents. He played the role of a father to my mother, who lost her parents when she was about three years old. He was a strict vegetarian, and my mother cooked and served his meals. He was a devout Christian and maintained his Indian culture to the end. This is part of what Uncle wrote in his history of the Havajees about his father: "He abandoned his ancestral property. He made your father and me promise that we would never claim or even accept it, even if it were offered to us. Before his death he made us promise him the same." They kept the promise.

Dad led the evening devotions, and his prayers were long and covered the world. He never failed to pray for the Jews and the United States. He always prayed that we would never be ashamed to stand up for Christian values. He meticulously tithed his income, and more, and had envelopes earmarked. At his death we found a stack of envelopes with names of organizations and monthly amounts, ready to mail for the month of May. He supported homes for widows, orphanages, leprosy patients. There was an envelope earmarked for the Jews that the church collected every Good Friday.

Dad was very health-conscious and made sure we always ate healthily. He was a great believer of homeopathic cures. He was mainly a vegetarian. He was highly intellectual and spent long hours with the books he ordered from the Standard Literature Company, Calcutta. After the first two years of college, Dad gave up higher education, obtained a diploma in commerce, and sent his brother and sister to college. His knowledge of world history, geography, and English literature was amazing. His friends were intellectual men, professors, freedom fighters, religious leaders, and others. Their discussions in our living room were lively. Dad purchased the first Philips radio in the neighborhood, and his friends dropped by at 6 PM to listen to the All India Radio Broadcast. Lively discussions followed. During World War II, Dad stayed up late into the night to listen to world news with a map of the world next to him. The next morning after he said the grace over breakfast, Mother joked, "Now your Dad will tell us what is happening at the Western Front." My sisters learned about the war and world affairs and often surprised their teachers.

Dad spoke English, Hindi, and Tamil and could read and write French. He worked for the British Steam Navigation Company. To supplement his income, he was a reporter for *Madras Mail*, a daily newspaper. We were not rich but never lacked anything. His humility and grace endeared him to everyone. We lived on a prominent road: All the dignitaries visiting our town drove past our house on the way to the governor's bungalow. The security police stood long hours until the motorcade passed. Dad took a thermos of coffee and handed cups of it to them. They were guards and policemen. Neighbors asked Dad why he did this, and he said, "I could be that policeman. Everyone in life needs to be appreciated." When he died, these men came to Mom to tell her how kind he was and how they missed him.

There were a few times when he left the dinner table and went into his room. Mother told us he regretted he had given only enough money for one meal when a poor man asked for alms. What if he had a family? When he sat at the table with plenty of food, he saw those stretched-out hands and those of the poor man's family. He felt a sense of guilt that he had not given more money. Every weekend the poor came by for alms, and there was money set aside. One Saturday, Dad was busy, and when a leper came to the door, he told me to give him alms. I threw the money into his bowl. Dad heard it and firmly reprimanded, "If this were your dad, how would you feel if someone were rude like you were to him?"

The night of April 13, 1967, Dad passed away peacefully from a massive heart attack. Two of my older sisters and their families were living in Calcutta and Hyderabad. My third sister and Mother were totally broken, and I had to be brave for their sake. At his death, we came to know of the influence he had with his friends of all religions. His humility, compassion, generosity, and the respect he showed to everyone were a testament to a life well-lived. To his co-workers he gave money when in need and did not expect repayment. Mother got after him when she found a little note with money from a grateful recipient. He always had an explanation, which of course did not satisfy my mother. An annual event was the mango season, which was in summer, when Dad ordered a special variety and personally gave some to each of his colleagues, including the security and cleaning staff. To Dad everyone was special. At dinner that night, he took a mango and thanked God for blessings of the past year. He invited his colleagues, including the support and cleaning staff, to tea on Christmas Day. These thoughtful acts made him truly great. My parents were planning to settle in either Hyderabad or Bangalore where they had their roots. My choice was to remain and continue to work in school. He built a house in Waltair Uplands and named it *Beulah*, which means "favored and blessed of the Lord" (see Isa 62:4). Our home was open to everyone, rich and poor, and people of all faiths. Later, the school moved to the vicinity of our home. When a cyclone hit our town, neighbors from the low areas came to our home, and our living room became a bedroom.

Dad was handsome and well-dressed. I remember the care he took to keep us all healthy. When he attended traditional Indian weddings, he wore a silk shirt and dhoti (a wrap around the waist) and a scarf with a gold border. He spent long hours reading his Bible and in meditation. He and Mother prayed together before lunch. A few days before he passed away, he told her that when he was gone, she would be alone and face criticism for letting me be single. He made her promise never to raise the subject with me. Mother kept her promise. When friends asked him what he would want if given another choice, he replied, "Eight girls and no boys!" He made us feel loved.

The night Dad passed away, at dinner a Hindu family asked him what his background was. Mother smiled at us because we knew what his answer would be. But he surprised us when he briefly shared his father's conversion and mentioned the family gothra (clan), "Atreya gothra," and that his brother was named Atreya Rao.

When I became a teacher, he prayed over me and gave me this advice: "Be who God made you. Do not compare yourself to anyone. Work hard and do your best. Sing the song God has given to you. Accept responsibilities without expecting rewards. Love breaks down walls of prejudice." He brought people from the ships from other countries to our home, and Mother served meals to them. I was scared when I saw a man from Africa in the living room and sobbed with fear. When he left, Dad drew a head with curly hair and said God loved people from Africa very much and God carefully made the curls. He told us everyone was special to God. When I traveled to Africa, I looked at the dear people as specially chosen by God.

Dad was forgiving and held no grudges. When the contractor of Beulah was producing wrong bills, Dad fired him, and the man took him to court. It was humiliating for him to be in court, as he was well-known in the town, and the attorneys sympathized with him. The judge's verdict read, "Men may lie, but books do not." Later, when Dad heard the contractor passed away, he wrote a sympathy letter to his wife. When Mother reminded him of how he was treated, his answer was, "Do you want me to go down to his level?"

Dad was very patient and loving. I do not ever remember him making a remark that hurt our self-esteem. All he said was, "I am your dad, and I love you and need to tell you what you just said is not quite right. Think it over. If you have any questions, we will further discuss the matter." The concept of "father figure" is very important to every child. I once read of a little boy praying, "God, Dad is mean to Mom. Please punish him but do not hurt him." Children find it hard to accept God as a loving father, all because of a harsh father.

Dad's mother was Havaji Jeeva Bai, daughter of Rev. Job Paul, who received his theological degree from United Theological College, Bangalore, in 1897 and was with the English Methodist Church. He translated the whole liturgy of the Wesleyan Methodist Church into Kannada, hymns and lyrics, and translated plays by William Shakespeare and composed stories for primary students into Kannada. He so impressed Rev. B. L. Rice that he made him the first Indian priest of what is now Rice Memorial Church on Avenue Road, near Cubbonpet, Bangalore. Dad's mother was a trained teacher and taught school.

My mother, Havajee (Indukuri) Mary Sowbhgyavathi Jeyaraja Rao, daughter of Vadlamanetti Venkayya (Brahmin Convert) and Indukuri Ratnamma (a Kshatriya convert), was born January 19, 1903, and died November 5, 1997.

When my mother married my father, as per the custom in his family, Grandfather named her Vijaya Bai. My dad called her "Vijji," and Mother called him

"Jeya," though it was not common in their day to call a husband by his first name. We know really nothing about my maternal grandparents. They gave up their earthly wealth when they became followers of Jesus. Their names are in the *History of CMS Telugu Churches*, a book I had lost. We heard Mother's maternal aunt was the Rani of Dummagudam, who went on horseback to visit her constituents. There is no way I can verify this, as women's names were not recorded in the history of Kshatriya community.

Mother lost her parents when she was three years old. Her eldest sister, Sundara Paul, wife of Dayaseela Paul, who worked in the Mint in Hyderabad, India, took her and her sibling and raised them in great luxury. When I was about ten, an elderly hawker brought saris, and while he showed the saris, he kept looking at my mother with tears. He asked her if she was a relative of Ratnamma Garu who lived in Eluru. Mother told him she is her daughter. He told her that he was a poor young man, and on a rainy night he was shivering with high fever and took shelter in the front porch of a certain house. Grandma heard his groans and sent a servant to find out what the matter was. She sent him some of Grandfather's clothes and a hot meal. He went in, thanked her, and told her he was poor and had no work. She gave him a few new saris to sell in order to make some money, and this is why he was now a hawker of saris. He saw the resemblance between my mother and her mother. Mother became very emotional as she saw her mother through him. Thereafter, none of us dared to tell her that she was too lavish because her answer was, "Like mother, like daughter!"

Dad and Mother came from different backgrounds, and their food habits were different: Mother loved rich, non-vegetarian food, and Dad was very traditional and a vegetarian. He was rather quiet while Mother loved fun. She was attractive and loved everything beautiful, which included a large stack of pure silk saris of all colors. At home, she wore crisp cotton saris and was always neat. She was generous, often extravagant, and lavish. When she married Dad, she did not know how to cook. She went to Dad's mother for a couple months and became an amazing gourmet cook. Her cakes and pastries were her signature dishes. My parents came from two different language areas and spoke English always.

Mother was meticulous in everything she did, whether it was cooking, sewing or crochet, or anything else. The home was always clean and tidy. She spoke to the plants and told them how beautiful their blossoms were. Both she and Dad loved flowers, and our garden was ablaze with color.

Mother had a child's heart, played games with us and with our toys. On Saturdays, she bathed our celluloid dolls and dressed them in colorful outfits she had made, and then she sang to them. Later, I brought her a toy from my travels for her toy collection. On my way to the Singapore airport, I dashed into a toyshop and the man at the counter asked how old my child was and whether it was a boy or girl. When I told Mother this, she said I should have told him it was for her! She had a melodious singing voice and filled the house with hymns and love songs. Her last Sunday on earth, she asked for a hymn-sing, and while her grandsons played the guitars, she joined in the singing.

Dad gave her a rosebud for her hair every day, and when he passed away, it was painful to see her passing her fingers over the rose bushes. A widow does not wear flowers in her hair. My mother's faith kept her strong over the loss of my dad and their daughter, my sister Rachel Suguna. Suguna and her husband had lived in England for twenty-three years, and when they retired, they returned home and lived in the house she had built adjacent to ours. Five months later, Suguna died of a drug reaction. One night, Mother was in prayer and called out to me and said, "I miss Suguna, but God does not make a mistake. He knows what he is doing." It was her strong faith in God that sustained her through sorrowful times. She never blamed God. Three times a day, she sat in her bed and prayed with her head covered. Arthritis in her knees prevented her from kneeling, and she kept hoping she would be able to kneel someday. She gave strict instructions that all telephone calls and visitors should wait while she was in prayer.

In April 1974, while at breakfast, she held my hand and said she had a dream that I was writhing in pain. She stretched her hand and prayed for me. I teased her that she was a dreamer like Joseph, but she insisted she was serious and made me promise I would go and see Dr. Leoni of St. Joseph's Catholic Hospital over the weekend. She reminded me Friday night, woke me up early on Saturday, and when the car was pulling out, she said, "Tell the doctor the whole truth!" The doctor was surprised to see me, and I told her the reason I was there. She examined me and found nothing was wrong, except that I could lose some weight! I asked her to put it in writing to relieve Mother's anxiety. She thought for a while and said that when Mother had had surgery for a strangulated hernia, the nuns had seen something special in her. So the doctor decided to do one more test on me. She found a large fibroid and fixed the date for surgery. Mother was relieved and thanked God for answering her prayer.

A reputed surgeon performed the surgery, and Dr. Leoni assisted him. Never discredit a praying mother's advice and prayers!

I called Mother often while I was abroad, and her concern was whether I was having timely meals and enough sleep. When I said, "Yes," her response was, "You cannot hide the truth from your mother!" At home I worked late into the night, often until dawn, with schoolwork and answering telephone calls and faxes that came from abroad. One night she pulled a chair and sat in silence while I continued to work. It was 2:30 AM, and I told her she should go to bed. She gently said, "I am not disturbing you, am I? I am looking at you and saying a prayer for you. I do not get to see you during the day because your first love is that blooming school" (she always used this word!). I hugged her, apologized, and got into bed, sobbing. A mother's love is unmatched! The elderly are not looking for gifts or luxuries but love and a little time with their family. I regret my being so busy and wish I had another opportunity to be more thoughtful.

During Christmas, Mama celebrated over the top. Her signature dish was a thirty-pound dark fruitcake: Dry fruit was soaked in brandy in September, the cake made in mid-December and sent with special instructions to the baker for baking. Anyone who dealt with Mother knew her high standards. On Christmas Eve with Christmas greetings, she sent out at least twenty-five large trays with eight or nine homemade treats along with a slice of fruitcake to friends and neighbors of all faiths.

She faithfully read her Bible and *God Calling*, a daily devotional. Prayer was a vital part of her life, and she always sang the old hymns from *Songs and Solos*. She was "the Queen of the House and High Command." She had a chair in the kitchen to supervise the cook and others who worked in our home. The outpouring of sorrow at her death from the rich and poor was a fitting tribute.

Mother was strong-willed. She fractured her hip in her mid-eighties but refused to use a cane or crutches. When she knew I got a pair of crutches for her, she firmly told me to donate them to St. Joseph's Hospital and said, "I will walk." She walked in two months and attended the sixtieth anniversary of the school!

A couple of days before she passed away, her system began to shut down. Her doctor visited her every day, often twice. Though she was a little slow, she did her morning chores and came out neatly dressed and hair in place. Our dear friend Sandy Wisener took care of her day and night; she was the only one Mother allowed. Several times she pulled the bedside curtain aside and with a smile whispered, "Jesus is the sweetest name I know." Sandy told me her death was near. I could not imagine life without her. The day she passed away I felt the need to stay home. She ordered me to get dressed and go to work. I stayed away from her sight. On November 5, 1997, with the family around her, she slipped away peacefully. Sandy prepared her body for the funeral the next day. She was draped in her favorite sari that she kept aside in her closet with the matching blouse. She was prepared to go. She shared Dad's grave. At the celebration of her life, the minister compared her to the wise woman in Proverbs 31, which was appropriate.

Birth and Childhood

Mary Jeyaraja Rao and her daughters

I was born in Visakhapatnam, India, the fourth girl, to Mary and Havajee Daniel Jeyaraja Rao. My three sisters are Hannah Saraswati Bai, wife of Edward Rajaratnam, an engineer who was sent by the government of India to New Castle upon Tyne to study naval architecture; Ruth Savithri Amala Bai, wife of William Rajaratnam (Edward's brother), retired as director of shipping, Food Corporation of India; and Rachel Suguna Bai, wife of Richard Calder, who both worked in England for twenty-three years.

When mother was expecting a fourth child, she prayed fervently that it would be a good-looking boy who could carry on the family name. It is important in the Indian culture to have a son. On July 4, 1930, the nurse announced, "It's a girl!" When Dad walked into the hospital room, he found mother crying and asked the reason. Mother told him that the stigma of not giving him a boy continued to worry her. Dad told her that every child, male and female, is God's gift and added, "What if she is taken away from us?" The very thought of losing her child scared her. They held hands and prayed, thanking God and accepting me as a special girl from God. I was a spoiled brat, according to my sisters, as in my parents' eyes I could never do wrong. The three sons-in-law were sons to my parents. When friends asked how he managed to live with five women, my dad would joke that we kept him in his place.

My middle name is Shakambari Bai, a name coined by my grandfather, a Sanskrit scholar. Its meaning, derived from Shaka (leaves), and Ambari (clothed), connotes a woman clothed with leaves (Eve). My grandfather told my parents that no one will have this name; indeed, I have not met anyone with this name. I was embarrassed, as no one pronounced it correctly and everyone made fun of me, as if I were an alien from another planet. While I was doing the bachelor of teaching, the principal called me to her office, and there were several of my teachers with her. She said, "Your name does not indicate your background. Who are you?" I explained. It was the coup de grâce, and I vowed it was the end to that name. When I returned home, I convinced my dad and dropped it from all my records. What is in a name? All that matters is what we do with our life. I regret that I let down my grandfather. Now I have a hard time living up to my first name, Mercy!

The town where I was born is located on the Bay of Bengal on the East Coast of India, where the beaches are wide and beautiful. A familiar sound was the drum beat of the town crier, who at the street corner announced important news and it spread through town. Most evenings the families walked together to the beach. Mothers exchanged recipes and whispered the latest gossip while the children played with water, chased crabs, and built sandcastles. The latter activity always ended in someone kicking a nice castle out of sheer jealousy. The culprit always cried the loudest, but no one showed sympathy as children make up for differences and hold no grudges. Our fathers went on long walks discussing politics. When we saw the keeper of the lighthouse go up the spiral steps and turn on the lights, it was time to go home. Dad told us the lights guided ships safely to the harbor and each one of us is a walking light who should help others from danger. When I hear the song "Brighten the Corner Where You Are," a hymn by Charles H. Gabriel, his words come alive:

> Do not wait until some deed of greatness you may do,
> Do not wait to shed your light afar;
> To the many duties ever near you now be true,
> Brighten the corner where you are.
> Someone far from harbor you may guide across the bar;
> Brighten the corner where you are.

Community is important in India. In pain, sorrow, and joy people come together irrespective of faith and background. There were no funeral homes. When someone died, the body lay at home until it was time to be removed to the cemetery or cremation grounds. Women, dressed in white, sat in silence with the women while the men sat outside in the yard to comfort the men. Church bells rang the tolls to announce the death of a member of the parish, and the passersby stopped with head bowed for a minute. Later, the church sexton brought the register to the parishioners with details of the deceased person and funeral arrangements. There is a close bond among people.

The Indian home is never quiet. Friends and family come by unannounced and are welcome always. Hired helpers who do household chores are extended family, and there is always extra food to serve them and the unexpected visitor. Hospitality is the hallmark of an Indian home. Grandparents, elders, and parents are highly respected, and when they walk into the room, children stand up to greet them with the typical Indian greeting, "Namaste." Unless told to stay, the children leave the room.

I am often asked if marriages are still arranged. There was a time when this was the norm. Parents desire the best for their children, so "research" of the background of the boy/girl is important. A trusted friend of the family often acts as a mediator to look into the financial soundness, genetic health problems, caste, and especially the character of the young people. Divorce was unknown. Marriages are "made in heaven" and should last until death. A formal engagement precedes the wedding. Weddings are expensive, and 200 to 500 guests, sometimes more, attend the ceremony and a lavish meal. On the third day the bride leaves for the groom's home, with her trousseau and several varieties of sweets and candies, which the groom's family sends out to friends to announce the arrival of the bride. At a reception hosted by the groom's family, the guests meet the new bride. The girl does have a say in the choice of her mate. Customs have changed, and intercaste and interfaith marriages are not an exception anymore as young people travel abroad for study and work and choose a mate.

Every morning, vendors would bring to our door farm-fresh vegetables, seasonal fruit, and a variety of leafy vegetables. There is a superstition that the first buyer brought *bhoni*—a social, commercial custom whereby the first sale of the day brings the seller luck for subsequent transactions during the remainder of the day. They believed my mother brought luck, and whether needed or not, they insisted she make the first purchase of at least one item. The vendors were part of our life as well as the poor that came to the door. A certain woman brought fresh eggs, and another brought fresh-roasted cashews. The one thing that greatly interested friends from abroad was to watch a milkman with his cow, milking it at the back door every afternoon. Mother supervised the process, making sure that the bowl, the udder of the cow, and the hands of the milkman were clean. The milk was strained and boiled. We always drank hot milk with Ovaltine twice a day.

Life once was lived leisurely, and the joke was it is "India Stretchable Time." Families had breakfast and dinner together. Very few mothers had careers. I always came home to find Mother there to greet us. This is not an absolute anymore. We played mainly outdoors. Every morning, Mother and Dad sat on the front porch sipping coffee with Kruschen salt, discussing the garden while Tommy, our dog, played in the yard. The oil bath was a Saturday ritual. Our ears were cleaned with sesame oil warmed and cooled with a pod of garlic; the body was soaked with pure coconut oil and massaged with a fine powder made with some ten kinds of herbs, dried red rose petals, and lots of pure turmeric powder. We had no hair dryers, and incense fumes from hot coals were fanned to dry our long hair. It was a long and relaxing process, but we refused to go through this when we became teens. Mother continued this every Friday, and her skin was beautiful until the end.

We were members of St. John's Church. Dad was a lay trustee and member of the synod. When the chaplain was out, Dad preached the sermon. He was an eloquent speaker, an intellectual with a good command of English. Every Sunday, we attended the morning and evening services and Sunday school. Infants were christened, named in naming ceremonies, and as teens confirmed in a commitment to discipleship by the laying on of hands by the bishop. Spiritually, this made no difference in my life.

War Years: World War II

War does not solve problems. War results in widows, orphans, lost loved ones, empty beds, and chairs.

Passenger ships to Burma left from the local port, and by virtue of his work, Dad knew several passengers. When Japan attacked Burma, women and children were sent back to India while the men stayed behind. The ships pulled in late at night, and Dad was present to check arrivals and documents. He heard women call out Dad's name, and it became a joke to his co-workers. The men had told them that Dad would help them connect with their families in India. Dad brought to our home those who had no family to meet them. Mother rearranged the living room and another room for them; after a hot shower, she served them a hot meal. They narrated the horrors they had faced.

April 6, 1942, was Easter Monday. We had just had breakfast when air raid sirens blared to announce an air attack by the Japanese. People scrambled to the trenches that had been built on all roads, and there was chaos. The sound of guns was deafening; our guests wept aloud, recalling what they had experienced in the past. Mother calmed them and shut all doors and windows. Two Japanese fighter planes flew over the town, and we learned later that the intent was to destroy the two ships in the harbor that were carrying ammunition to the Allied troops in Burma. The ships fired at the aircraft, which dropped three bombs as they flew over them. Fortunately, they did not explode. The town narrowly escaped major devastation.

Later, five Japanese aircraft flew over the town. We had a shelter in our home—a large dining table surrounded with sandbags. Several nights sirens warned us of an attack, and the family rushed downstairs to hide under the shelter. I was a heavy sleeper and slept through everything, oblivious to the fact that my parents carried me down to the shelter and took me back to bed when the all-clear siren blared. My sisters teased, and my dear dad told them that mine was "the sleep of the innocent."

Things took a serious turn. Families living near the harbor were aware of the impending danger, and we spent a week at an uncle's farm on the outskirts of town. We later went to a nearby village where Dad's cousin was a veterinary surgeon. Dad came for the weekends. When my uncle was posted out of the city, we moved to another village and rented a local pastor's thatched-roof hut, which had dirt floors and kerosene lamps. The simple and healthy lifestyle of the people kept us happy. I was particularly happy because I did not have to attend school! Later we moved to a larger home that had electricity!

As a child, I was fragile and often came down with high fever. A draft of chill wind or a "strange" face triggered this. I was terrified of sailors who got off the ships, and there were brawls in the liquor bar that was next to our home. I was extremely fearful of doctors and hospitals. When I was four years old, Mother had a hysterectomy and was in the hospital for twenty-one days. Dad took us to see her every afternoon. I sorely missed her and cried as she waved to us. I decided that hospitals and doctors were out to get my mother! This fear still lingers.

When I was five, I developed a double case of typhoid, and two specialists offered no hope of my survival. It is a miracle that I am alive. The recovery was long, and I had to learn to walk and digest solid food. I was lanky and awkward in my movements and was sensitive to remarks like "She is ugly," especially by my teachers. I heard them say I was not like my three beautiful sisters. I was not selected to any play or dance. What I went through helped me show extra love and attention to children who carried layers of hurt and were aloof and suspicious of others. It takes just a word or remark to ruin a child's confidence.

Education

I was a year older when admitted to Standard One of Queen Mary's Government School for Girls. My parents wanted us to grow up with girls of all faiths and backgrounds. I got a double promotion and skipped Standard Two. I cried every morning for five years about having to go to school and envied the servants who had a free life! My sisters disowned me once we entered the school. We did cursive writing right from the start. The teacher told us our handwriting "reflected our character," and we believed her. I hated school and swore I would never be a teacher!

My mother often told me I was a tomboy and "Girls do not do this." I did not ask why, as I knew the answer: "Because I told you so." Two of the teachers I frustrated had passed away, and when I met my needlework teacher many years later I apologized to her. She told me I was a good girl and was no trouble to her. She added, "The girls of today are not obedient like you." I am glad she had a short memory! This helped me to say an encouraging word to my students.

My best friend in Standard One had lost her mother. The teacher was calling out words, and we were writing the spelling. I spelled the first word and wrote it on my friend's slate. Teachers have a way to find out the one who errs. Our teacher told us to put down our slates, and she came around to check the word. When she recognized my handwriting, she gave me a tight slap. I ran out of the class crying and threatened to tell my dad. I did not know that my dad was on the school board! I am not sure what I told my mother, but that evening my teacher came to our home and apologized to Mother. I felt like a hero until my parents warned me never to act "smart" or disobey teachers. I never complained again, as I had gotten a double dose from them. That's how sassy I was as a child!

A Memorable Year: 1947

On August 15, 1947, India became an independent nation after 200 years under British rule. At midnight the British flag came down, and India's tricolor flag went up on the flag mast. There were celebrations in the country and in our school. Dad raised the Indian flag in our home, prayed for the prosperity of the country, and thanked God for freedom and for those who peacefully and nonviolently obtained it. He also told us that each of us had a special role to play to make India great. At school there was a grand celebration, and we proudly saluted the flag and sang the national anthem, composed by Nobel laureate Rabindranath Tagore.

On August 24, 1947, my grandmother, Havajee Jeeva Bai, passed away. She and my aunt, Havajee Kaveri Bai, retired headmistress of girls' schools, were spending the summer with us when my grandmother had a paralytic stroke and lost her speech and the use of one side of her body. For three months Mother took care of her as a dutiful eldest daughter-in-law. This took a toll on her, and we were concerned. My eldest sister had just read Isaiah 38. King Hezekiah was very sick and dying. He prayed for healing and length of days. God spoke to the prophet Isaiah that he heard the king's prayer and he would extend his life by fifteen years. That night my sister heard a voice that Mother's time was up. She prayed Mama would live, and so did we. As it happened, Mother lived to be two months short of age ninety-five and did not die until November 5, 1997. God heard and answered our prayers.

Grandmother's was the first death in the family that I remember. Like others in Dad's family, Grandma was brilliant. She had explained to my two older sisters Shakespeare's plays, Milton's *Paradise Lost*, and other classics of English literature. She once asked me to read to her chapter 3 of the Epistle of James, which talks about the evils of the human tongue. Her explanation helped me put a lock to my lips (though not always!). She taught me to spell "VIBGYOR," the seven colors of the rainbow. I was proud to be the only one who could spell and name the colors of the rainbow in grade three. She was a trained teacher and worked in several government schools in the state, including the school where we studied. Her death left many unanswered questions: What happens after death? What are heaven and hell? Is there a God up there, and how does God know me? Does God care? Where is my grandmother? Will I see her again? I often watched the sky and looked for her and heaven.

October 31, 1947, marked the beginning of my spiritual journey. Our family was devoutly Christian. Daily devotions and church attendance were a part of our life. My grandparents on both Dad's and Mother's side left their Hindu faith and earthly possessions to embrace the Christian faith, and I felt entitled to a place in heaven. God was distant and angry, keeping score of the wrongdoings of everyone. A friend of my dad's, an evangelist, came to town to conduct revival meetings, and Dad took the family to introduce us to him. A couple of young people testified to the change Jesus had made in their lives. In his message the preacher compared the human heart to a calm and beautiful volcano until it erupts and destroys everything around it. This analogy clicked. I was happy on the outside, and people said my name should be Joyce, but deep inside there was a void. I realized for the first time that there is more to life.

For three days I wrestled with whether the time had come to turn my life over to Jesus. On the fourth day I prayed, "God, *if* you are God, speak to me. If you don't, I will never bow before you." That was a daring prayer, but my loving God sent the spirit of conviction. I wept, confessed my sins (which I did not think were sins), and saw myself as a lost soul. Anger, lying, pride, and stealing money to buy street food were prohibited by Mom. I did not consider them sins and did not know that is how sin enters one's life. I confessed my sins and sought God's forgiveness. A burden lifted, and peace took its place. When I got up from my knees, a doubt arose: Was this real, or was I imagining? I asked for something tangible. I heard a whisper: "Read Isaiah 6:7: 'See, this has touched your lips; your guilt is taken away and your sin atoned for.'"

Life took a dramatic turn. People experience the "new birth" in many ways, and there is no uniformity. Your personal experience should not discredit the experiences of others. "By their fruit you will recognize them" (Matt 7:20). My teachers saw the change in my behavior. The headmistress of the school, who was not a Christian, sent for me and asked what had changed in my life. I shared my testimony, and she responded, "I wish I had that experience." I often prayed for her and was happy when, a few years later, she came to inspect the school where I was a teacher.

Except for Dad, the rest of us gave our lives to the Lord, and Dad told us we were carrying our beliefs too far. Mother prayed a lot for him, and when he got home from work on a Saturday, he told Mother he could not fight the truth and to pray for and with him. They went into their room, and when they came down, Mother told us that Dad had turned his life over to the Lord. We, as a family, began the new spiritual journey together in seven days.

I had a deep desire to tell everyone what God did in my life, and on January 5, 1948, I prayed earnestly that God would bid my parents to adopt a son who would be a missionary and I would support him! I expected God to put his stamp of approval on my agenda. I heard the familiar voice: "Mercy, I want *you* to go to the ends of the earth for me." I made several excuses, but the voice persisted: "Read Jeremiah 1:1–9." I was surprised to read, "Do not be afraid of them." How did God know this? I argued, struggled, and at last said, "Yes." I knew I must grow spiritually; I read the Bible on my knees and prayed a lot. My sisters and I went to women's college dorms for Bible study and prayers. I spoke at local women's meetings. My passion was to see women become leaders in their own setting. It was not until 1960 that this became a reality. I learned to be faithful and serve God where I lived.

God's Call to
Be a Schoolteacher

When I graduated from high school, I joined Mrs. AVN College, a local co-educational institution, for four years of undergraduate studies. I graduated with honors and was awarded a gold medal for English literature. It was my wish to have a master's degree and a doctorate in English. We were away on a summer vacation, and I missed the date to submit my application in the local university. I was angry to have to wait another year. I thought then that I had made a fatal mistake when I said, "God, what do you want me to do?" His response shocked me: "Mercy, I want you to be a teacher!" Me, a teacher? Why did I seek his will? After a long battle, I surrendered my will in exchange for his. "'For I know the plans I have for you,' declares the LORD, 'plans to prosper you and not to harm you, plans to give you hope and a future'" (Jer 29:11).

How do we know when God speaks? His voice is gentle and kind; he knows the purpose from the beginning to the end and is never critical. My dreams went up in flames, and his dream emerged. It was a life-changing moment, and I headed in a new direction. There was one setback. Dad did not want us to become professional women. After graduation, two of my sisters worked as teachers and got married. When I told him of my new plan, his response was, "It will not happen." On the second day, he told me that he and Mother had prayed, and he said, "You are a special child, and if God is leading you in this path, we will send you with our blessing." With that, he blessed me. I went to Lady Willingdon Women's College in Chennai to pursue a bachelor's degree in teaching. To be away from home and to share a hostel room with two other girls was a new experience. I spent the weekends with my sister and her husband, who lived in Guindy, and returned with a package of snacks on Monday morning. I went home only twice during those nine months.

Anglo-Indian Protestant Middle School

Just before my final examination, I received a letter from Dad that Miss Hellyer, the Canadian manager of the local school run by the Canadian Baptist Mission, had offered me a job. Dad had made it clear to her that I would not be interested in teaching. This did not deter her. One Sunday she confronted him and asked him why a Christian father did not want his daughter to work in a Christian school. Just to "get rid of her," Dad wrote, "he had left the decision to me." I was shocked and could not consider working in a small school that people referred to as "Rabbit Warren." The day I arrived home, Miss Hellyer rang our doorbell and walked in. Sometimes God *does* have a sense of humor. She was happy I was back and asked if I would report to work the following Monday! My tongue was tied. How could I say no to a foreign woman who had given her life to serve the needy children of my town? Forty-eight years of sheer joy and fulfillment awaited me.

The school was housed in the Sunday School building next to St. John's Church. Three medium-sized rooms were for grades seven through nine, and three small rooms were for elementary grades. Two classes were handled by one teacher. This was a stark

Timpany Senior School

contrast to the large girls' school I had attended, where students were from different religious and economic backgrounds.

On July 1, 1954, my career began as teacher of grades four and five for a monthly salary of Rs. 120/= (US $24). That day I looked around and revolted at the thought of working in that setting. The first three nights I wept and could not imagine continuing there. My mother asked the reason and told my Dad.

He apologized, told me to tender my resignation the following day, and said he would pay any dues I owed the school. I was thrilled and mentally composed the letter. I could not sleep that night and decided to talk to the Lord. I heard the gentle whisper, "Mercy, I want you to build a work for me in this school." Did I hear correctly? How does anyone build a work in a school, especially this school with seventy students on its rolls? I questioned and doubted but finally submitted to God's will. I asked for just one thing: that I might have a deep love for the students at this school. How right God is and how wrong I was to question him! The following morning, I surprised my parents with my decision, and Dad made it clear that the decision was entirely mine and not his. I had perfect peace when I entered the school and began my work with the precious children.

The concept of "building a work for me" was confusing. I understood later that it was to build lives in integrity and right values so they would make a difference in the world, which they did. I am proud of my students, who are spread all over the world and credit the school for making them who they are today.

Then and now, I never considered myself an educator in any official sense of the term. I just fell in love with children. I had no business or organizational skills and worked untiringly with the few resources the school had. My heart was passionate about teaching and working. I went to God on my knees and learned a lot from the Bible. Its principles and truth sustained me through troubled times. I sought no fame or worldly pleasure—my world was small and my needs few. I made myself available to God and to the children, to instill in them the truth that there is nothing to live for when integrity is lost. Jesus chose twelve simple men in whom he invested his time and love, and he empowered them to carry his message to the world. Two thousand years later, lives continue to be changed through the life-giving message. My Bible continues to be a gold mine, and the more I dig into it, the more I am blessed. The best time to get still before God is the early hours of the morning, while it is yet dark and birds sing their joyous songs and bring hope and cheer. Time spent with God continues to equip me to go through the day.

Growth of the School

Mercy's Academic Leadership Team

The enrollment of children steadily rose in number from seventy boys and girls. I was thrilled when the number rose to 120 students in one year. The applications for admission from Indian students steadily increased. The school catered mainly to Anglo-Indian pupils, and the Department of Education prescribed a minimal ratio for admission of Indian students. The rule was soon relaxed, and admission was open to all, irrespective of caste, faith, or social status. We did not give in to pressure from those who felt entitled because of their status or religion. Parents who doubted the results of their child's performance could see the answer scripts. Every child is a gift from God and has no choice where he/she is born. Soon the word spread that we would not give in to threats or fears.

The present building was bursting its seams, and we built four additional rooms on the property of Union Chapel. The growth continued. The Canadian Baptist Mission built a larger building on its property in Waltair Uplands, Visakhapatnam, and the school moved into it. God was fulfilling what he said in 1954 about building a work for him. On the day of registration for admission at the new location, early in the morning parents lined the two roads leading to the school. The traffic police called to say that traffic was held up and asked that something be done to clear the roads. The staff worked long and hard to expedite the process.

Currently, former students of the school are in about forty countries. We are proud of them as they continue to make a difference where they are located. There is a beautiful bond of friendship, and they come together from around the world for reunions. They hold high the ideals of their alma mater. Why was it a co-educational school? I studied in a girls' school and found it difficult to fit into a co-educational college. We made a conscious decision to be a co-ed school and to receive no funds from the government or from any agency. Students paid a small fee, and the staff worked for lower salaries and invested their best to prepare students to be world citizens. I took no vacation and spent that time organizing for the new academic year. My dad often told friends that my "one and only love" was the school. On January 1, 1959, I became the first Indian headmistress, and my monthly salary went up by five dollars. My needs were few as I lived at home and my social activities were few. All I needed was to work for my children. I had a lot of administrative work in addition to teaching English literature to the top two classes.

Additional courses were offered by the school, and it was rewarding to see the results of these special courses:

1. The Center for Special Education for children with special needs was opened in 1964. It was sad to know that some of them had not seen the outside world, as the belief was that the family was reaping the consequences of their past sins. The way these precious children blossomed was amazing. The love students showered on them was heartfelt, and they often brought gifts and birthday goodies to them. Two teachers were sent by the school to be trained to teach these children with special needs.

2. The school also offered personality courses to women for a couple of years.

3. Adult education was offered for all support staff.

4. English classes in Steel City School were offered for mothers of students and interested ladies.

Timpany School Society

All of us can plant a tree for someone else to water or write a song for someone else to sing. Paul saw it this way: "I planted the seed, Apollos watered it, but God has been making it grow" (1 Cor 3:6). God gets all the glory.

My administrative work increased in addition to teaching English. The school offered three sets of electives to prepare students to pursue graduate degrees in engineering, medicine, or arts. We were the first school to offer computer science as an elective subject and got the approval of the Indian School Certificate Examination. Two parents from the Indian Institute of Technology helped to formulate the curriculum, and later the examination board introduced it in other schools in the country. I took a brief course in order to operate it and had basic principles (only). I put up a good front, and they believed I knew it all! I listened with keen interest but had no clue what they were saying. I am glad they asked no questions. We were thankful for the help, which added a new dimension to the school.

My children taught me more precious lessons than I taught them. Given another chance, I would be a teacher and nothing else. It is a great experience to make an investment in young lives, and the school is proud of preparing outstanding men and women.

In 1968, as the Canadian Baptist Missionaries were leaving India, Timpany School Society was formed. A group of nine members, eight plus myself, were given the responsibility for the leadership and direction of the school.

The Asian Baptist Women's Union

In 1958 I traveled to Calcutta for a Women's Continental Conference from Asia. Outside the Lower Circle Road Baptist Church, the noise from the streets was deafening. Women from thirty-five war-torn Asian countries came together, bearing deep scars of sorrow, pain, and suspicion. The ice began to melt the very first night. On the second day the air cleared. Women shared their experiences of torture, starvation, prison, and the death of loved ones shot in their presence in spite of their pleas. No eye was dry. Women from the offending countries walked across the aisle, hugged each other, and sought forgiveness. God's spirit was visibly at work: "Love one another. As I have loved you, so you must love one another" (John 13:34). As women held hands and prayed, we felt we were standing on holy ground. Only God's spirit can bring healing and reconciliation to hurting hearts. Mrs. Martin, president of the Women's Department of the Baptist World Alliance, brought an emotional speech, calling the Baptist women of Asia to tear down the walls that separated them and to love and forgive each other. Her love and concern to unite us were a direct call from God.

The words of the hymn "Sweet, Sweet Spirit" best describe our experience: "There's a sweet, sweet Spirit in this place / And I know that it's the Spirit of the Lord / There are sweet expressions on each face, / And I know they feel the presence of the Lord. Sweet Holy Spirit, Sweet Heavenly Dove, stay right here with us, filling us with Your love."

What began with doubt, fear, and suspicion ended in lifelong friendships. We were "one in the bond of love," breaking all geographical barriers. The final parting was emotional, as women locked hands and with tear-stained faces sang: "Blest be the tie that binds." I was elected vice president of the newly formed Asian Baptist Women's Continental Union (ABWU), serving in that capacity from 1958 to 1963. Later, I served as president of the ABWU from 1988–1993.

How did I become a Baptist? After our new spiritual experience in 1947, Dad told us that he had been a nominal Christian and wished to make a public confession of his new spiritual journey by baptism by immersion. The local pastors were not willing to baptize us, as Dad was a well-known Christian member of the Church of England; as such, it would result in strained relations in the churches. When Brother Bakht Singh, a world-renowned Sikh evangelist, came to town for gospel meetings, he agreed to baptize the family. The following Sunday, when Mother and Dad went for the morning service, the Scottish chaplain told them they could not partake in the Lord's Supper. Dad was visibly hurt and returned home after the first part of the service. Later, we received a letter from the bishop, informing us that the family was excommunicated from the Church of England. Since my parents had limited knowledge of the local language, we joined Union Chapel, a Canadian Baptist church, where the services were in English. This is the reason I was invited to the conference in Calcutta. Little did I know that this was just the beginning of a long journey around the world from 1960–2000.

Union Chapel, The Family's Church

While eating breakfast the last day before we left Calcutta in 1958, I wrote these words:

> The winds are laden with greetings
> As they blow from East to West,
> The dream has come true,
> our labors blest.
> Calcutta hummed its usual activity,
> But within her portals a structure of rare magnanimity,
> "Asian Baptist Women's Union"
> Was formed with sweet communion.
> Women of Asia had met,
> God on them His seal did set,
> Under the banner of the Crucified.
> Hand in hand stood they
> And pledged themselves in unity,
> To work together, to count no cost
> To keep His Light bright in the East.
> They know not what the future holds.
> Enveloped, may often be, among dark clouds.

But not for long, they will soon drift,
His smile to reveal as the mists lift.
The last link in the chain of gold
Has at last been fixed to hold,
East and West together, to work, to love, to conquer
Marching forward in His power.
We pledged to "Work Together with God"
Down through the ages this record will hold
For future generations His love to behold.

—Mercy Jeyaraja Rao

I composed and read this poem to the women of the ABWU after I had given them a message on Esther.

For Such a Time as This

"Called for Such a Time as This," said Mordecai
"I'm not called," said Esther.
Esther and her maids prayed, she cried,
"If I perish, I perish. I will go to the King."
Like her, I said, "Not for me, this honor, Lord,
My fears are many. I'm not the one, Lord.

"The path is steep, oh, so rough.
The odds, Lord, are against me.
No royal throne awaits me…
No crown shall ever be mine,
Beautiful, I'm not, dear Lord,
Not me, Lord, find another."

The Master, gently whispered,
"You are Mine…the Price I paid,
The debt is cleared. Rejoice, my child.
It's my grace…Calvary's grace.
Rise! Go to the ends of earth,
Fear not, I'll go with you."

"Called at such a time as this."
I'll arise and take my place.
God's woman at work, I'll be,

Not in my strength but the One who sends me
Get me out of the way, Lord,
To you belong glory and praise. (Esther 4:14)

—Mercy Jeyaraja Rao

On the occasion of the seventh assembly of the ABWU, Jakarta, Indonesia, July 1988, I challenged the women with the following words:

"Daughters of Asia, arise." Hear His call,
"Who will go for Me?
My message to share and My work to do
My Kingdom to build,
And reach the lost and lonely?"

"At a time such as this,"
Like Esther of old, Will you arise,
And go to your King…
"If I perish, I perish
My people I will serve."

Renew history, be a Deborah,
Defeat the enemy, overtime he works.
Call thy people together
Cry out, "Now is the time of action,
The Lord leads us on!"

Are you saying…"Lord, I'll go…Send me."
Consider…commit…arise. Go…
To love as He loved, "Even unto death."
To pray as He prayed, "Not my will but Thine,"
To go as He said, "Go, into the whole world."

Called to commitment and growth, arise!
Together we will work
Together we will pray
Together we will claim,
"Asia for Christ."

—Mercy Jeyaraja Rao

The Baptist World Alliance–
Women's Department

Mercy at her 70th Birthday Celebration

I received an invitation from Mrs. George Martin to attend the Baptist Women's Leadership Conference and BWA World Congress in Rio de Janeiro, Brazil, in July 1960. I was sure my dad would not agree to this, and I left the letter on his table. He handed it back and said to send my regrets immediately. He also said to tell her that I would not travel out of India! Mother whispered to me that they would pray and not to respond yet to the letter. Is this what God spoke to me on January 5, 1948? Should I obey God or my dad? On the third day, Dad told me he and Mother accepted me as a special gift; over the years God was using me, and they would not go against God's will for my life. There was great pain on Dad's face. Dad contacted Quanta Airlines as to the cost of the round trip from India to Rio and back and the cost of a round-the-world trip. The difference was minimal, and so we worked out details and stops. I had a big stack of tickets and visas to travel to the Middle East, Europe, Great Britain, South America, the United States, Canada, and Asia. My plan was a three-month trip, which turned out to be eleven months.

Brother Bhakt Singh came to town, and I told my parents not to mention my travels to him since I knew his stand that women are to minster only to women. On a previous visit to our home, I had questioned him as to what women should do if the Lord called them to bring his word to a mixed crowd, and he said, "He will not." Mother reprimanded me for questioning a great man of God! He visited our home, and Dad asked him to pray for my travel and told him I would be away for three months. He prayed with them and said it would be longer than three months. He came by the school, and I wondered what I would say, in case my parents had told him of my travels. Some of the staff went to him for prayer, and I was hoping he would leave, but he called for me! After prayer, he told me the following: I would be speaking to both women and men. God's call was not to tell people about my culture to entertain the audience. People have spiritual needs, and God's Word has answers, and I was to share only what God laid on my heart. He told me not to accept remuneration for speaking, as money could become a snare. God would take care of my needs. I was also not to limit my travels to three months. God would lead me when it was time to return. I am grateful for his advice. People did invite me to talk about worldly matters, including television programs. I declined. I did not accept remuneration, and it saved me from the temptation of shopping, especially at Christmas!

A few weeks before I left home, I had a moment of doubt and confusion. I saw a letter from Dad's evangelist friend. I froze at the contents. He wrote that I had taken the wrong train, was traveling in the wrong direction, and added words of caution. Was I disobeying God? I ran to my room with my Bible and the stack of tickets. I prayed that I would cancel my trip and would God please show me his will. I opened my Bible. I do not randomly open my Bible to find an answer, but I was desperate. My eyes fell on this passage of Scripture from the book of Job: "I thought, 'Age should speak; advanced years should teach wisdom.' But it is the spirit in a person, the breath of the Almighty, that gives him understanding. It is not only the old who are wise, not only the aged who understand what is right. Therefore, I say, 'Listen to me'"(Job 32:7–10).

Yes, we can go directly to God, who hears and answers prayers. "Call on me in the day of trouble; I will deliver you, and you will honor me" (Ps 50:15). "Ask and it will be given you; seek and ye will find; knock and the door will be opened to you" (Matt 7:7). I do respect and seek counsel of the wise who will tell me truthful answers.

How do you know when God speaks? God's Word is our standard and reference book. He will never lie and go back on what he said. Take time to listen to him, and be willing to obey him. God, who is truth, will never lie.

World Travels, 1960–1961

The day dawned to leave home to go into an unknown world. As I knelt before them, Dad prayed an emotional prayer while Mother and Rachel shed tears. Mother always sent us away by putting a cross on our forehead. The one consolation was that Jean Palmquist, the Canadian manager of the school, was traveling with me. As the train pulled out on its way to Calcutta, it was a tearful parting. Jean and I boarded the flight at Calcutta and met up with three friends all bound ultimately to Rio. The first stop was Beirut, where a missionary couple met us and at lunch briefed us on our travel through Jordan and Syria. Later, I spoke to the students of the American University. We set off in a cab to Damascus and on the way stopped at several checkpoints to have our passports checked. At one place, the man held up our five passports from five countries and said, "United Nations!" Late that night we arrived in Damascus and checked into a third-rate hotel, the only place available. The next day, the cab driver drove us to some historic places, including the window from which St. Paul was let down (Acts 9:25). We traveled to the Holy Land, a sacred experience to walk where Jesus walked, taught, healed, forgave, wept, and performed miracles. We dipped our feet in the River Jordan and knelt in prayer in the garden of Gethsemane, where Jesus prayed (Matt 26:36–46). We attended a communion service and partook of the sacred elements symbolizing the broken body and shed blood of Jesus. We walked into the empty tomb and stood speechless—the Lord of the earth lay in a simple borrowed tomb. The guide said, "He is not here; he has risen, just as he said. Come and see the place where he lay. Then go quickly and tell his disciples: 'He has risen from the dead'" (Matt 28:6–7).

At Jacob's well we relived Jesus's conversation with the Samaritan woman (John 4:7). We thanked God for Jesus, the crucifixion, death, and resurrection that brought to the world the message of redemption and release. Since that visit, the Bible continues to come alive every single day when I read it. Our next stop was Rome, and we visited all the historic places, including the Vatican.

Jean and I flew to Seville, Spain, to visit friends and proceeded to London. We enjoyed the tours since we read British history in school. Jean flew to Canada and I to Rio de Janeiro alone. If I could have, I would have returned home!

Rio de Janeiro

Mercy in Rio

While I waited to board the flight, I felt lonely stepping into new territory and with a long journey ahead. The flight attendant, seeing my tears, tapped me and said, "It will be okay," and was extra kind on the flight to Paris. The flight to Rio was long and tedious, and I was grateful to have two vacant seats beside mine to give vent to my loneliness. I was unprepared for what I experienced during my stay in Rio. I drew a lot of attention because of my sari. The following day, my picture was in the local newspapers with the caption, "A woman wrapped in yards and yards of material arrives in Rio." There was another picture in a magazine in which I would never have chosen to appear. People gathered to get a glimpse of me and shake my hand. Seeing this, four Canadian women accompanied me every time I left for the meetings. I was once coming down the platform when a man handed me a packet of coffee beans, and the next day my picture was in a newspaper as advertisement for coffee. None of this is a reflection on the dear people of Brazil. They are warm, loving, and hospitable. A woman in a sari was a rare phenomenon.

The one experience that reshaped my prayer life happened my first Sunday in Rio. I walked into a rundown church building to bring God's message and sensed a sweet spirit. What I write is according to my interpreter. The pastor introduced me to the congregation and shared the story of the church. Several years ago, an elderly woman, who cleaned wealthy homes, prayed for the young women who were doing similar work in the neighborhood that they would know Jesus as their Savior. Some of them came to her, and they gathered under a tree to study the Bible and pray. More joined the group, and they prayed for a meeting place. A neighbor gave his garage, where they met for services and prayer meetings. The present building was like a large barn. The numbers increased, and they pledged to forgo buying new clothes and to give the money toward the building fund. It was a cold morning, and they did not have many warm clothes. What would I say to these dear people?

The service was over, and as I was hurrying out to be in time for the opening of the Congress, an elderly man walked up, held my hand, and this is the gist of what he said: Thirteen years ago, he heard about India, where many people did not follow Jesus, and he had prayed every day for India. That morning, he asked the Lord to show him at least one person from India in heaven, as he did not expect to see one this side of heaven. There I was, and he looked up and prayed: "Lord, thank you for answered prayer. I am ready to come home to you." It was a hallowed moment and reminded me of Simeon's prayer when he saw Jesus in the temple (Luke 2:29–32). It was thirteen years after he prayed for India that revival broke out in my hometown. Was it not an answer to his prayers? This gave my prayer a new dimension. Pray faithfully even when you do not see the answers to your prayers.

United States and Canada

I flew from Rio to Miami with Mrs. Marie Mathis and Miss Alma Hunt, two great Baptist women. I went on to Baltimore at the invitation of Rev. and Mrs. Garland, who were Canadian Baptist missionaries in my hometown and good friends of my parents. It was a refreshing time, especially to eat Indian food prepared by Mrs. Garland. It was there I first saw an apple tree with fruit. On my first Sunday in the United States, I brought the message at First Baptist Church, Baltimore, where Rev. Garland was the pastor. I made copious notes to impress the American congregation! When I stood up to speak, I got confused, put them aside, and spoke what God had laid on my heart. After the service, they gave me an envelope, which I knew was payment for the message. The purpose of my travels was to share God's Word, not to receive money. My travel expenses were paid in advance, and I often stayed in homes and had no other expenses. My dad sent me money for personal expenses from time to time through friends who came to America.

My speaking engagements involved a lot of travel, and the schedules were hectic. I had spoken at the Annual North American Baptist Women's Union at Ridgecrest, and the morning I was leaving for Washington, DC, I woke up with excruciating back pain. When my friend, Edna Woofter, came to pick me up, I got into her car with great difficulty. A heavy schedule of speaking awaited me in the United States and Canada. Edna took me to a kind doctor who ordered heat treatment, and I wore a heavy back brace. He warned me that back problems often require multiple surgeries. God answered the prayers of my parents. It is sixty years, and the problem has not recurred. It is a great blessing to have praying parents.

I spoke in about twenty-five states. I loved the women, and they loved me, a stranger. Sometimes men were in the women's meetings, and it was okay.

I traveled from coast to coast in Canada, speaking often. It was an honor to reconnect with Miss Laura Bain, the founder of Timpany School in 1931, and to thank her for her vision for children of India.

I had a full taste of a snowy winter and snow boots! Very often, I got off at the airport, not knowing who would meet me. I trusted God, who promised, "Do not fear, for I am with you" (Isa 41:10).

My second visit to Canada was after I had the problem with my back. I flew to Toronto via Washington, DC, and New York on a very hot day with my back brace on. I was hurting. While waiting for the flight to Toronto, ready to cry, I opened my Bible, which I always carried, and expected to read something uplifting. It was anything but comforting. My eyes caught these verses: "I am a stranger on earth" (Ps 119:19). This was not what I needed, and I quickly turned the page, hoping for something more comforting! "Your decrees are the theme of my song wherever I lodge" (Ps 119:54). Yes, I was a stranger and a pilgrim on unknown terrain!

On arrival, my baggage did not arrive. My host gave me her nightwear, and I bought toiletries. In the next few days, I was to speak at a women's conference at McMaster University, Waterloo, Canada, where the women were beautifully dressed, mainly in purple. Here I was in the same clothes, and I wanted to tell them that my bags with gorgeous saris had not arrived. The Lord fixed my pride and seemed to say that I was not there to display my clothes but to share God's Word. When the bags did arrive after four days, the conference was over, and I was happy to have all my clothes.

There are many memories that bring a smile to me after these many years. While flying to Birmingham, Alabama, I felt a hot liquid on my sari. The airline hostess apologized and said she was admiring my "dress" and got distracted! The man at the cleaners looked at my sari and wrote, "Long tablecloth"!

My first Christmas away from home was in the United States, where I witnessed two events. The first was the lighting of the national Christmas tree in Washington, DC, on December 23, 1960. It was an awesome experience to be physically present as President Eisenhower lit the Christmas tree. The second was the inauguration of President John F. Kennedy on January 20, 1961. My friend got tickets for both of us to attend, but the previous evening, as I was returning after speaking in Baltimore, Maryland, there was a blizzard, and the next day the streets were slick and dangerous. We watched it on a color TV at a friend's home. To view it on TV was a good substitute. President Kennedy's much quoted call to service, "Ask not what your country can do for you; ask what you can do for your country," is a powerful message. Yes, rewards are earned and are not an entitlement.

I continue to smile at some of the things people asked me: "Do you have electricity in India?" "You poor thing from a poor country, where people are hungry and famished, how did you get those white teeth?" "Is the filigree pendant in your chain an Indian god that you once worshiped?" "What is your tribe?" I was waiting at the auditorium to speak to high school students when one of them asked me who I was. I said, "An Indian." He looked surprised and said, "No! You don't got no feathers!" After that, I told people I am from the country of India. "Have you eaten a cake?" "Where did you learn to speak English? Do you speak through an interpreter?" While introducing me, a friend asked a group of children, "Do you know where our speaker is from?" "From heaven," said one child. A friend shrieked with fear when she walked into my room at night and saw my white teeth and brown face! "Are you a queen? Does part of the material wrapped around you include a hat?" "What do you wear under this 'long tablecloth'?" At some airports, passports were stamped and handed back while boarding the flight. At one airport, when I heard the officer call out "Hayaraha Row," I was amused and wondered who would have such a strange name. When he held up my passport and I went forward to collect it, the look he gave me implied, "What else do you expect from one who does not know her name?" We live to learn! Incidents such as these do break the monotony, especially when you are tired.

Was I offended? No, these incidents reminded me that people in India also have many unanswered questions about people from other countries: Why are their eyes blue? Is she a teenager? If not, why is she wearing a "dress"? Why don't they use their fingers to eat food?

This is less true now since people freely travel to other countries for advanced studies and for work. Television plays a major role in bridging the gap.

Asia

I flew out of San Francisco to Honolulu, Hawaii, where I spoke a few times. I went on to Tokyo, where I spoke to women and children in a school. The women hosted a formal Japanese tea ceremony. The grace, love, hospitality, and dances of Asia are colorful. I had the first taste of a steam bath from hot springs in Japan! My visit to Hong Kong was busy with speaking engagements there. Our cultures differ, but we form a beautiful tapestry woven by the hands of our God, the master weaver.

I was away for eleven months, and then I boarded the flight to Calcutta. I wondered, "What now?" I asked for two things: that I would not be proud and boast about my experiences and travels, and that I would speak simple Telugu when invited to speak at Telugu speaking conventions. God answered my prayer. Telugu is the regional language of my state. Since my parents were from different language-speaking states, they spoke English. I wished to express God's Word in simple and plain Telugu to everyone, educated and uneducated. God did answer my prayer and helped me address thousands of men and women in my state in Telugu.

A Tale of Two Women

In 1994 I received a fax from the Baptist World Alliance Women's Department (BWA–WD) that I was being given a designated scholarship to attend the Baptist World Alliance Congress in Buenos Aires, Argentina. I faxed my regret. I could not leave my mother so soon after my sister's death. One night, Mother asked if I was putting her first, before the Lord's will. Her question was direct: "Can you not trust God to take care of me? You must obey the Lord." I confessed what I had done, and she held my hand and prayed that I would obey God. I then faxed my consent and received a form for the position of president of BWA–WD. My qualifications were simple and few: I had a deep desire to encourage women to take up leadership positions in their respective countries. Meanwhile, I had accepted an offer to serve as vice president of the BWA. The day I arrived in Buenos Aires, the search committee interviewed me. I served as vice president of BWA and president of BWA–WD, 1995–2000.

This was an awesome responsibility, and I depended on God to keep me faithful and safe. I also wanted to build bridges for men and women to work together as co-laborers with God. Yes, every day I prayed that God would lead me one step at a time and sang to myself: "One day at a time, sweet Jesus, that's all I am asking from You. Lord, help me today, show me the way, one day at a time." I am grateful for my parents, family, and friends, who prayed for me and encouraged me.

Mary Hutson

My days were so full with press and TV interviews in Buenos Aires, Argentina, that I did not ask who was the donor of the scholarship. After the Congress was over, I found out that Mary Hutson was responsible for it. In 1960 I had been the main speaker at the Arkansas State Woman's Missionary Union Annual Convention. Mary was the director of youth work in the state. She prayed for me for thirty-five years. She got the women of the First Baptist Church in Knoxville, Tennessee, where she later worshiped, to pray for me over the years and to put together the scholarship for me. The last thing Mary did at the morning service at First Baptist Church, Knoxville, in December 1994, was to present the check to my predecessor, Catherine Allen. The following Monday, Mary went to the doctor for a checkup and found out she had advanced stage liver cancer. She died on January 4, 1995. At the celebration of her life, which was held on an icy, cold, snowy Friday night, hundreds of people from all walks of life gathered to express their gratitude and love to this humble servant of the Lord. Mary loved and accepted every person she met, and she lovingly served, especially those who were down and out and unnoticed by others. Sandy Wisener, to whom Mary was a spiritual mentor, wrote these words in celebration of her life:

> Mary Hutson, citizen of the world, lived a life among us with gentleness and strength. She was revolutionary in her living and counter to our culture in her values while cherishing the tradition of her faith and her church. Mary ministered in positions within the church and Baptist denomination at Central Baptist Church, Fountain City; First Baptist Church, Knoxville; Arkansas Baptist Woman's Missionary Union; and Tennessee Baptist Woman's Missionary Union. In addition, without title or position, she ministered through her love of people in ways unnoticed except by those she touched throughout her pilgrimage.
>
> Mary loved beauty and helped those around her to appreciate the natural beauty of the world. She also saw and was active in her concern and passion for the hungry, the homeless, those heavy of heart and spirit, and those who experienced the pain of being human. Mary's life was no brief candle; it was a splendid torch she held not for a moment and made it burn brightly before handing it on to future generations.

In gratitude for Mary's spiritual guidance, Sandy set up a Mary Hutson Memorial Fund with the BWA–WD for my travels and to train women leaders around the world who would build God's kingdom in their own cultural setting. Mary Hutson's vision may have been similar to the perspective of Henri Nouwen, who wrote in the book *The Road to Daybreak: A Spiritual Journey,* "Community requires a lot of patience and a willingness to let others do slowly what you can do rapidly. It always means choosing a work in which people much less capable than you can participate. It asks for a deep inner conviction that a slow job done together is better than a fast job done alone" (Doubleday: New York, Kindle edition, 1990).

Sandy Joins Mercy at 70th Birthday Celebration

Sandy Wisener

Sandy Wisener came into my life as a special gift from God through Mary Hutson. In Mary's final days, Sandy was caring for her, and Mary assured her that she would not be alone and that she would be closer to her than she had been in life. In a mystical and miraculous way, God brought Sandy to India. She was one of four national managers of the operation component of Ernst and Young's Health Care Consulting Practice. They had no international health care practice. Suddenly, they decided to expand internationally, to begin in Asia, and they asked Sandy to come to Asia to develop the strategy and to begin the practice. By very unusual circumstances, her firm sent her to India midway in her travels and research of the Asian market.

Mother's simple faith, trust, and practical Christian living left indelible impressions on the family and every life she touched. When Sandy was coming to visit me in India in May 1996, Mother, who had never met Sandy, said to me, "The woman who is coming is an answer to my prayer." "What prayer?" I asked. Her calm reply was, "She *is* the answer to my prayer. What I am saying to you now, you will not understand, but soon you will." The day Sandy arrived in our home, Mother went to her room and told Sandy that she had prayed for me for years that when she died, God would raise someone to take care of me, and Sandy was the answer to her prayer. "This is your home, and you are a part of this family." This surprised my family. Mother loved Sandy and felt she took

Rachel's place. Her song returned. A few weeks after Sandy's arrival, Mother went home peacefully to be with the Lord. In William Cooper's words, "God works in a mysterious way, His wonders to perform." God's promises are true: "'For I know the plans I have for you,' declares the LORD, 'plans to prosper you and not to harm you, plans to give you hope and a future'" (Jer 29:11). I am grateful that God, who called me to a new ministry and a new community, gave me a new friend and companion to make it easier to follow that call. Sandy traveled with me after she retired.

The joy of our friendship is that we both deeply feel that God put us together in answer to the prayers of two Marys—Mary Hutson and Mary Jeyaraja Rao. We have seen how this deep bond between two strong women from two backgrounds and continents allows us to be a help to each other, to grow closer to him, and to work together for the women of the world. God has prepared Sandy for this ministry throughout her life. When she was young, and before having a successful business career, God took her to Nigeria, Brazil, Ethiopia, and Guinea Bissau to work in hospitals, villages, and leper colonies, as well as to meet and work with heads of state. God has given her a heart to understand and relate to people from many different backgrounds and a desire to build community. In Luke 10 we are told the Lord sent out his disciples "two by two." We, too, are created and equipped by God and sent out to serve.

World Travels, 1995–2000

Women are a gift from God to bless every generation. Women blessed my life. (I am withholding the names of the countries while I write the following experiences.) War and poverty did not destroy their trust in God or their love for people.

The women of a certain country requested that we give them three months' time before the executive director, secretary-treasurer, and I visited. The reason was to enable them to save a portion of their ration of rice and beans to feed us. They grew no vegetables and raised no chickens, because if they did, soldiers would vandalize their yards. Their homes and churches were dilapidated. The simple meals were very tasty because love and sacrifice were the main ingredients.

The hotel room we shared was big enough for three beds with a small bathroom and three little bars of soap. The friend who took us to the airport collected the bits of soap for the women waiting for them at the entrance; this was the only soap they had. Children in the churches sang hymns from memory, as they could not afford hymnals. None of these circumstances killed their faith and love for the Lord. People filled the church and waited outside to listen to the message through microphones. The scariest moment was when, at departure time, my passport was retained after it was checked. I was told to step aside and was guarded by two armed men. I claimed God's presence and peace. Just before departure, I was escorted to the aircraft, and the men handed me my passport before the doors closed. I came to know later that the dear women who came to see us off prayed for my deliverance on their knees. "I have engraved you on the palms of my hands" (Isa 49:16).

In another country, the poverty of the people and marks of persecution for their faith were evident everywhere. The first morning was bitterly cold, and we rode in an old cab and did not realize that the three of us were fast asleep until we reached the destination! God protected us from death by the fuel smoke. A large crowd of women gathered, and when I was speaking, I saw the angelic face of a woman who was taking notes holding the book close to her eyes. I asked the interpreter if she needed a pair of eyeglasses. No, she did not want glasses; she was content and happy, as poor eyesight brought her close to God, and she had a telephone ministry and prayed with people who called. She turned her adversity to a blessing. The following Sunday she handed me a box of chocolates for the "mother who gave you to the world." She prayed over me for safe travels. Mother was touched with the gift and the story of the giver.

My travels around the world have taught me precious and sacred lessons. I was speaking at a women's conference in a war-torn Eastern European country. At lunch, an elderly woman handed the interpreter a piece of pie. She was a widow with a meager pension who faithfully tithed, saved a couple of dollars to make pies for the homebound poor women, and shared the gospel. I noticed her tattered shoes and gave my interpreter some money for a pair of shoes. As she took it, she turned her eyes to the ceiling and prayed, "Lord, I did not ask you for this. Let me wear out the new shoes by serving you." Oh, to be grateful for every blessing we receive!

I was in another country where the effects of nuclear explosion had left serious illness and death. I was speaking to young people who were receiving treatment for cancer. It was heartbreaking to see beautiful infants in the arms of their mothers waiting at the doctor's office. It was not easy to tell them that God is a loving God. When the meeting was over, several of the children came for a hug. Three of them followed me, and one asked, "Is it wrong for me to hate someone who has both parents. I am an orphan. Do you have parents?" I was saddened and told her, "Hate does not solve problems, and God is with you and loves you." She then said, "Please take me to your home." That look still haunts me. Do I understand? Do I care? Where do I begin? Do I know what it is to be sick and lonely in the world? There were pregnant mothers stricken with cancer waiting to hear their diagnosis! As we were driving away, there was that same girl seated on a rock waving to me! Did she wonder why I was unconcerned? Do I complain over trifling matters? Is there something I can do for the lonely, the sick, the abandoned? What is the role I can play?

On a visit to Seoul, South Korea, my friend pointed to the red lights through my window. There were hundreds of lights. It indicated that people had gathered to pray in churches until midnight. At the crack of dawn, the lights were back on and people had already gathered for prayer. Prayer blesses individuals, families, and nations.

Retirement, Old Age, and Angels Unaware

I was once young, and now I am ninety. Length of life is in God's hand, and each day is a gift from God. What are the lessons I value? Never knock down anyone in order to advance yourself. Let no one shake your faith in yourself and God. Truth will ultimately triumph. Life is a battle, and the weapons of our warfare are strength and trust in God. We must overcome evil with good. Never hold grudges, as they eat into your soul. God is the only one on whom you can depend. Trust him, love him, be faithful to him, talk to him and listen to him. God and the Bible have been my stay and anchor when storms raged. As a child I sang, "With Christ in the vessel I can smile at the storm"; this is a reminder that God is faithful. God understands and cares.

I retired on March 31, 2002. The three schools had dedicated and committed principals and staff, and I had no doubt they would take the schools to greater heights. I was still the chair of the school board and planned to travel back and forth. Sandy, true to the promise she made to Mama, brought me along with her to the United States, and we moved into the large home she built

Mercy and Sandy at 70th Birthday Celebration

on the Tennessee River. In early July I received a call from India that the schools were taken over by a certain individual with the help of the police and judiciary and that the top personnel had been dismissed.

Sandy and I traveled to India, and when we landed in Mumbai, a friend met us and warned against proceeding to Visakhapatnam, as there was a "plot" against us. We checked into a different hotel, and I lay limp in bed while Sandy was on the telephone for many hours talking to caring friends. It was late evening when she said, "Get up. Have a shower, and get dressed. We are returning to the United States in a little while. Ask no questions." I had trusted her intuitions and judgment in the past, so I got ready. On arriving at the airport, the flight crew was surprised to see us back; we had flown on the same flight with the same crew, and they now made available two seats for us for the return trip. We both collapsed into our seats and fell asleep until the announcement that we were descending into Atlanta. We saw the flight attendant clean the canteen area with a brush she carried in a bag. When she passed by, we thanked her for her dedication to her work and said, "God bless you." She said, "I watched both of you since you boarded the flight and felt guardian angels were watching over you the whole night while you slept." Were we hearing right? She gave us her business card, and this was on it:

Watchers in the Night

There is rest in God's promise to protect you. He makes this promise out of His perfect love and endless mercy toward you. He is ever present, always caring and constantly watching over your life. May He keep you safe in the arms of His love today. "For He will command His angels concerning you, to guard you in all your ways." Psalm 91:11

She knew nothing of our situation, but God used her to encourage and remind us that we were not alone in the situation we were facing. In the words of the song, "[God's] eye is on the sparrow, and I know he cares for me." What a difference a smile, a word of encouragement, and a blessing make in the life of individuals! Oh, to be a blessing to someone, every day!

Are there angels "unawares"? We once flew to Houston to be with a loved one for her surgery. At the airport car rentals, the woman who handed us the papers asked us where we were going. When we told her, she said, "I will pray for you. God be with you." As we drove to the hospital, we missed the right exit. An elderly man in a white car stopped and asked where we were going. When we told him, he said, "Follow me. I know the place." He directed us and got down from his car and said, "I have led many to this place. It is a good place." Before we could thank him, he left. Was he an angel unaware? The surgery was successful. "I Believe in Angels" was one of Mama's favorite songs!

In August 1995 Sandy came into my life. She visited us in India, and in 1996 she made our home her base as she traveled all over Asia for six years. When mother passed away, Sandy was my rock. She stood with me through all the fiery trials I faced and saved my life. In April 2002 we came to live in

Knoxville, Tennessee. Since then, her home is mine. She worked untiringly for eleven years for me to become a U.S. citizen. She filed all the necessary papers, and I became a citizen on October 3, 2013. God and she continue to bless me. I live a peaceful life and a life of leisure. God bless people like Sandy who love God, love people of all cultures, and who keep the promises they make.

Part Two

My Career
as an Educator
1954–2002

Would I choose another profession if given the chance? My answer is "nothing but a teacher." Each moment of the forty-eight years I spent with children was sheer joy.

I began as a teacher in 1954 and became a headmistress in 1959. "New brooms sweep well," as the saying goes, and I decided to make some major changes. There was an undercurrent of resentment among the teachers. The reason was not because I was young and several of them were older with more experience, but the way I went about being a headmistress. The manager called for a meeting at which the teachers complained that many of my suggestions were not feasible. I made note of their concerns and apologized to them. Thereafter, we became friends and worked as a team.

The school grew in numbers. The Canadian Baptist Ministry (CBM) built a large building about eleven kilometers from the current building. Later, they also gave us the general bungalow of CBM, which was across the road. It had a couple acres of land, and we moved the kindergarten and primary classes. A new building was constructed for a second high school, Timpany Secondary School. At the request of the city officials, and to meet the need for a school in the industrial area of the town, a third school was constructed a few miles away from the town and became Timpany Steel City School. To commute among the three schools daily took up a lot time. The caring and well-trained leadership and staff who headed the schools had a deep desire to build the lives of the future generations.

In addition to excellence in academics, students participated in sports, cultural activities, and interschool competitions. Our students always brought home trophies. The naval band added flare to the annual interhouse athletic meet. At the end of the program, flags were brought down to the sound of "The Retreat," and at sunset a lone bugler played "Abide with Me." The annual Christmas cultural program was also a community event. At the end of the program each year, the manger scene depicted the rich and colorful culture of India. Some of the tableaus contained the typical dresses of each state: men and women, wedding dresses of a bridal couple, the professions of India. The choir sang Christmas carols. The most impressive program was children dressed in costumes of the world, locking hands and singing "We are the World." It was a beautiful moment to celebrate the world God had created and the beautiful people that fill it.

School Stories

Every year the school celebrated Parents' Day and Grandparents' Day. Grandparents traveled from other states to witness the children's exhibits in the classrooms and the special entertainment. Children composed a special song in their honor and wrote thank-you notes to them. This event brought the generations closer.

In 1955 the school flag was designed by Sylvia Gasper, a middle school student, with the motto "Seek Truth." I composed the school song in 1962:

Timpany School Song

We're of Timpany School
"Seek Truth" our golden rule
With open hearts and minds so free, our lofty goals we seek
And we are being trained to keep our lives unstained
And grow to be our country's best
And leave behind the rest.

Ch: We will work, we will play
We will help build every day
A school where deeds of truth are sown
And the Savior's love is known.

"Persevere to Conquer," "Progress to Perfection,"
"Undaunted ever scale new heights"
For wisdom thirsty be
We'll hold our banner high
For all that we aspire
Come, join our song of triumph loud
Of Timpany we're proud.

I looked forward to seeing the bright faces and hearing the sweet greetings of students. It was a hallowed moment when all of them repeated the Lord's Prayer every morning with hands folded. They sang melodiously hymns and songs.

The students had many names for me: Miss/ Principal/Princi/Big Miss/Jazz. They made me feel loved whatever they called me.

The first morning of every academic year, I told the schools the story of "the little engine that could." In one classroom a mischievous boy disconnected the intercom so they could not hear it! Years later at a reunion, he reminded me that he literally froze when I caught him in the very act. He dreaded the outcome. I smiled and said, "You are good at disconnecting, and please connect it!" It was fun to keep them guessing for the unexpected! It was a lesson he never forgot. Discipline is not necessarily harsh words, but a gentle rebuke drives home the lesson.

There is something very special about children. Love, discipline, encourage-ment bring out the best in them. Little wonder that Jesus said, "'Let the little children come to me, and do not hinder them, for the kingdom of God belongs to such as them. Truly I tell you, anyone who will not receive the kingdom of God like a little child will never enter it.' And he took the children in his arms, placed his hands on them and blessed them" (Mark 10:14–16). Love them. Teach them. Tell them they are a special gift from God and he not only loves them very much, but he has his hand on them for something special. What we say and how we behave leave a lasting impression on them. A professor of mine reminded us that children are like "wax to receive, marble to retain." What an awesome task is ours! Our words and actions are being heard, and characters are formed and built accordingly. God help us that we are never a stumbling block to children.

When the Canadians left India, they bequeathed me a soft leather strap. It was really "the proverbial strap." The fact that it was there helped with the discipline. I used it sometimes when a child repeatedly caused problems. It turned out to be a joke. A teacher brought four mischievous boys to the office, and when I gave the first boy the strap, he blew it off. The kids, the teacher, and I giggled, and they returned to their class like heroes and announced that the principal laughed and sent them away. Another boy returned to class and announced, "My dad hits harder; Principal is not strong." Thereafter, the strap disappeared, but the fear remained!

Randomly, I checked the shirt collars, shoes, and socks of the boys and girls to make sure they were clean. Long hair for boys was in style, and a few of them decided to followed suit. After two warnings, they were sent to the barber close to school with money for the haircut paid by a support staff. They had to bring the money to repay that staff member the next day! I warned them also that I would give them a "ceremonial haircut" before the whole school if they disobeyed. One boy dared me and said, "I want the ceremonial haircut." I was in a fix and tried to get him to obey. No, he would not, so I cut a wee piece of hair in the presence of his classmates! He asked for the hair and proclaimed, "Principal gave me a ceremonial haircut, the only one." I expected his parents to complain, but they did not. When I next saw him, he had a cleanly shaved head! We hugged and smiled! No love was lost—those precious children still love me and thank me for the discipline that shaped them to be who they are today!

Children learned that appearance, behavior, and personal hygiene are important to everyone, especially at the time of an interview. It amuses me that, decades later, former students visit me well dressed, their nails cut, clean collars, shoes and socks, and remind me that the training they received in days long ago has kept them in good stead. Discipline with a good dose of love yields rich dividends and produces outstanding citizens. A child who is never corrected or disciplined could be a disappointment. "Start children off on the way they should go, and even when they are old they will not turn from it" (Prov 22:6). I am grateful to understanding parents who knew the value of discipline.

September 5 is celebrated as Teachers' Day in India in honor of Dr. S. Radhakrishnan, who was a scholar and philosopher, first vice president and second president of India. It was his desire that instead of celebrating his birthday, it should be celebrated as Teachers' Day. The students of the top grades took over running the school day. At the end of the day, they planned a program for us, and one was mainly to imitate us! We saw ourselves through the eyes of our children. No feelings were hurt, and we thoroughly enjoyed ourselves. They left a thank-you note, telling us they appreciated our labor of love and also realized that it is *not* easy to be a teacher!

There were competitions between students and staff for major games that brought us together. Students were happy to beat us, but sometimes we beat them, and they joked that they played "soft" so we could win! A child's eyes have the power to speak volumes what is felt in the heart. A little love goes a long way and builds self-esteem. We told our children to dream big, work hard, and achieve their dreams.

One year on India's Independence Day, August 15, we drew the map of India, depicting the existing sixteen states, in chalk on the play field. On the outline and the states were little children seated in white dresses. A narrator described each state's culture, and older children danced, typically dressed in the costume of the state. That afternoon, it started to rain heavily, and the play field was flooded. Guests called to ask if the program would still be on. Hesitatingly, I said yes. I went to the three floors to see how the kids were. They were all dressed and looked downcast. As I was coming down to announce the cancellation of the program, a Hindu boy said, "Miss, please pray!" I felt rebuked, returned to my office, and prayed over the intercom that the rain would stop. When we said "Amen," the rain stopped, and I heard this boy shout, "Principal prayed, and it stopped raining." The PE teacher, a crew of staff, and captains of the school got the grounds ready, and the guests arrived. The performance was a great success. The sun was so fierce that by the end of the program, the one side of our faces was sunburnt! A board member joked that that happens when we pray to specify details to the Lord! At the morning assembly the following day, I told the children that it was not the "principal's prayers" and that everyone can pray, as God answers prayer. Former students tell me that the miracle they witnessed helps them to pray in faith in times of difficulty.

We soon received a second answer to prayer. I was in the office of the municipal commissioner when he received a telephone call. He told me the call was to inform him of the dire water situation and that educational institutions may be closed. I picked up courage to tell him that my children will pray for rain, and he gave me a look of disbelief. I returned and wrote, "Send us the rain, Lord; send us a lot of rain. We need the rain, Lord," and requested the principals to sing it with the children. That evening there was torrential rain, and my telephone was constantly ringing with calls from parents that their kids were jumping with joy that God answered prayer!

Prayer is a powerful weapon, and children learn that God answers prayer. Jimmy was a student in second grade. After the mid-morning break, he complained that something was biting his foot. The teacher took the shoe off, and a small live scorpion fell out. She exclaimed, "Oh Jimmy, you are not stung!" Jimmy said, "Every morning before I leave for school, Grandma prays for us. Jesus answered her prayer, Teacher!"

A friend of ours passed away, and at the celebration of her life, her daughter told us that every day in her lunchbox, her mom slipped a little note telling of her love for her. Now she is a mother and does the same for her twin children. I often wonder if the little boy's mother prayed for her son as she packed his lunch that morning! He gave it to Andrew, who gave it to Jesus, who blessed it and distributed it to 5,000 hungry people, and there were leftovers (Matt 14:13–21)! Things do happen when we pray!

Dark Clouds over the School

Life is never always easy for anyone. A leader has to be willing to climb the steep mountains of hardship, face insults, and wade through muddy waters of hatred and accusations. There is no turning back, as there is no armor for the back. In Ephesians 6, Paul explains this. The hymn "I Have Decided to Follow Jesus" was composed by a man in Assam, NE India, who became a follower of Jesus Christ. The village chief called on him to renounce his faith. He declined to do so, and threats to his family resulted in his wife's murder. He sang, "Though no one joins me, still I will follow…the Cross before me, the world behind me…I will follow Jesus" while being executed. His death was not in vain. The chief and others became Christians.

During my travails, friends and family covered me with love and prayers. There were a few times when I felt like Jacob, who said, "Everything is against me" (Gen 42:36). He cried out that Joseph was dead and he may lose Benjamin. Little did he know that Joseph was alive, second in command to Pharaoh, and that he would soon go to Egypt and would see Joseph. Yes, my God *is* alive and took me through fiery trials; all I had to do was, like David, find "strength in the LORD" (1 Sam 30:6).

The local newspapers reported false allegations. Sadly, most of them came from a few in the Christian community.

What were the allegations? (1) That students from the Christian community were not given preference in admissions; (2) that bribes may have been given by parents who held high positions in the city! They doubted that the admission process was open to all students, irrespective of who they were. The answer scripts were graded by a team of teachers and were always open for parents to review their children's answer scripts if they felt an injustice had been done; (3) that the majority of the teaching staff and students were non-Christian.

All this did not deter me from doing what God entrusted to me, and I was solely answerable to him. I would be absolutely useless if I had received anything unlawfully from anyone. I would have lost respect from staff and students if I were a bribe taker. In fact, when wealthy students brought candies on their birthdays for staff and fellow students, I normally gave them all to the support staff!

The fact that the schools were taken over when I retired and was out of the country does speak volumes to the question, "Why not when I was still working?" However, I have given that chapter of my life to the Lord Jesus and refrain from seeking reasons and answers.

I believed firmly that admission to the school should be open to everyone and not restricted to any one community. I had to be strong and hold my head high with a prayer that my children would not lose their trust in God and in humanity. Students and staff left notes of encouragement during the period when false allegations were in local papers. For a brief period of time, three members of the school board made the decision to curtail my official duties except my teaching assignments. The reason? None of them had educational backgrounds and wanted me to run the school like a factory. One morning, a teacher handed me Thomas à Kempis's book *The Imitation of Christ* with a marked page, and it was what I needed. A few others peered into my room to encourage me. This was just for a few months. It was reported to me that some parents questioned the board members and demanded that I should take back my usual duties, as they were not comfortable with the changes. I was not aware of this until much later. It is in times of trial that you know who your real friends are. The wound is deep when those you hired and mentored turn against you. I know what it is to be betrayed and ignored. "The wounds I was given at the house of my friends" (Zech 13:6). Why did I not walk out? It was for the sake of the parents who trusted their children to the school. A former board member once reminded me, "Lightning strikes the tallest tower." "If God is for us, who can be against us?" (Rom 8:31). Yes, there were anonymous letters with threats of death. It is always a coward who resorts to this. God, who called me to build a work for him, was with me.

February 10, 1987, my staff and I prepared the school diary and sent it to the printer. That evening while I was in prayer, the printer called to say that the chairman of the school had called to cancel the order and had said not to print anything I sent her and that he was the one in charge of everything! He was not an educator and had no clue about children and their needs. I told the printer to do his bidding. Gritting my teeth, still on my knees, I said loudly, "I am done. I will hand in my keys and walk out first thing tomorrow." Of what I prayed thereafter, I do not recall. My Bible was open before me, and I saw a verse that was marked: "If a ruler's anger rises against you, do not leave your post; calmness can lay great offenses to rest" (Eccl 10:4).

I smiled, and late at night I asked myself why I would mark that verse, and I looked it up again. The highlight was not there! The following day the printer called to say the materials would be ready on time! I asked no questions. When God is at work, leave it to him to take care of our problems and hurdles. I forgot the insults and accusations I was facing when I entered the schools and heard the cheery greetings of children.

Leaders have to fight fierce battles and still hold their heads high. They are not alone on the battlefield as God is with them. God has not called us to be "loners" or to be an island; we must surround ourselves with praying people. Do you know why someone who had no part in building an institution takes over the work you built with "blood, sweat, and tears"? Greed for money and power is the motive, but no one can steal your labor of love. "Her children arise and call her blessed.... Let her works bring her praise" (Prov 31:28, 31). Truth will ultimately succeed, though it may not always be in your lifetime. Greatness does not belong to us. I am an ordinary vessel but have an extraordinary God. To God belongs all the glory. Like Julius Caesar, we say, "You too, Brutus?" It hurts when the very ones whom you loved and helped turn against you. Accept this as what everyone faces, and with prayer and trust in God, continue the work God has entrusted to you. How true are the words of Frances G. Crosby in her hymn: "Not for ease or worldly pleasure / Not for fame my prayer shall be. Gladly will I toil and suffer / Only let me walk with Thee [God]."

How did deliverance come? A group of non-Christian parents of the school filed a case in the court. The investigation resulted in all the charges against me being dropped. I stood tall in the town when I returned to India in 2009 and attended two reunions hosted by students in my hometown Visakhapatnam and in Bangalore, and I hosted a luncheon for the staff of the school. The elite of the city and former parents of the schools' students hosted a grand reception. God forbid that I should ever steal glory that belongs to God! Let us remind ourselves of a verse of the following song: "In His time, In his time / He [God] makes all things beautiful / In His time / Lord, please show me every day / As you're teaching me your way / That you do just what you say / In your time.

Was it all work and no fun? No, I had lots of fun. Some students asked such things as: how old I was; do I ever cry; what do I do when I get home; do I dye my hair? No, I did not then! Is there an intercom in my home, and can I hear what they are saying? My answer was, "Yes!" The reason was a girl complained that a boy called her but did not tell her who he was. The word went around the school, "Principal has an intercom in her home and can hear everything we say!" All calls stopped. I doubt that this "trick" would work now!

For several years I invited students of the senior class to spend the day in our home. My parents enjoyed having them and enjoyed their pranks. Mother personally served them. One of them told everyone, "Principal is like any one of us!" It was a surprise to me. This boy later lost his life in the battle of Bangladesh, and the school held a brief memorial service. His dad sent me a picture of his glasses and other articles; it was hard not to sob at the sight of them. We lost another in the World Trade Center attack. A similar service was held for her. It hits you harder when some of your own "children" volunteer to defend their country and lose their lives. Let us find ways to help the families through tragedy.

After forty-eight years spent in school, I officially retired on March 31, 2002. I began as a primary school teacher, first Indian headmistress, principal and correspondent, executive director and general director. Was I perfect? Was I always right? Did I never make a mistake? If given another opportunity, would I do better? Yes, I would. Do I have regrets? Of course I do. The dark clouds of insult and humiliation made me stronger to serve the school to the very end. Was my labor in vain? I have lived long to see the success of the children who once walked the corridors of the school. Thank you, my precious boys and girls, for helping me to be who I am today—God's grace and you! Thank you, too, for keeping in touch with me and sharing your joys and successes. I am grateful to the parents for cooperating with the school. They were involved in the performance of their children's progress in school. Schools cannot do it alone.

Reunions and Voices of Former Students

The work of forty-eight years was not a futile effort. Students often wrote, "Where are you, Miss? Come back." One boy said he slipped to the Founders Hall every day and prayed for me standing before my portrait. The night is the darkest before dawn—it is not always darkness. "When I am afraid, I put my trust in [God]" (Ps 56:3). A child's heart is a precious treasure, and their insights and emotions are amazing.

At the farewell function for the graduating class, parents, students, and staff shed many tears at the very thought of parting. Yes, we would miss them and would love to walk with and protect them from the hurts they will face, but this privilege is not ours.

Former students write to share their memories of their time at school. The morning assembly talks have played a major role in their life. One wrote that every day he sings "Blessed Assurance, Jesus Is mine" and prays St. Francis of Assisi's prayer, "Make me an instrument of thy peace." Another with health issues sings, "My God is so big, so strong and so mighty. There's nothing my God cannot do." Some other favorite songs are "Great Is Thy Faithfulness," which was the school hymn; "Count your blessings"; "In God's green pastures feeding by His cool water's lie, Soft in the evening walk my Lord and I"; and "Have Thine own way, Lord." Training and molding lives begins early. Like the tender branches of a plant that can be easily bent and yet keep their form, so disciplining a child early with lots of love helps mold them.

I was surprised to receive a long letter from a student two decades after he left school. He was working in another country. He wrote that he had always resented me because I was strict. I had noticed this when I taught his class. It was midnight when he wrote, and it dawned on him that his success in life was due to the school. We are good friends now and keep in touch. "Cast your bread upon the waters, for after many days you will find it again" (Eccl 11:1).

One day I received the sad news that one of my students had passed away. He had been a doctor in Algeria. Earlier, when he had visited me, he touched my feet, wanting my blessing. This is a custom in India. Students seek their teacher's blessing by touching their feet, and the guru places his/her hand on the person and prays a blessing. He shared with me that one night he was tired and discouraged at work, and he heard my voice over the intercom calling his name and saying not to be afraid because God is with him. He called me "Amma" and Mother Teresa and asked me to run a clinic for which he would volunteer his service! I will miss him.

Along with their teachers, I accompanied high school students to Nepal. We visited the historic places, and one evening we went to a shopping mall and saw shopkeepers going in. There had been riots on the streets a few weeks before, and when the shopkeepers saw a group of students, they were concerned. I clapped to call attention to students and warned them to be kind and quiet. One of

the students called out to me that a former student of the school was in Katmandu on an official visit and asked the students if they were from Timpany School. He said, "That is the characteristic clap of Miss Jeyaraja Rao." It was humorous and amazing! As we hugged each other and recalled his time in the school, our students stood in awe! Memories are precious and bring a lot of joy.

Selecting Marble for the Chapel Udaipur

In December 2001, we had a four-day celebration for the school's seventieth year. Former students and staff joined the celebrations. The highlight was the opening of the school chapel. I often dreamed of the day a place for prayer and meditation could be created. It took Sandy to make it happen. She put in at least

Chapel at Timpany Senior School

ninety percent of the funds for it. We went to the marble hills at Udaipur, Jaipur, and personally selected the choicest marble. The marble mural depicts Jesus holding sheep. It was Mama's favorite picture. The one who sculptured it received the president's award for art in 2000. He attended the celebration and attributed the honor to the mural of Jesus.

April 27, 2007. The Blessings of Discipline: This was written from a former student, Krish Dhanam, who became a motivational speaker. After he addressed business executives in the local jam-packed colosseum, he wrote,

Have you ever looked back through the window of your past and questioned the necessity for some of the moments of your childhood? Have you ever paused to wonder if grade school was really needed? Have you ever second-guessed the disciplinary action of an authority figure and wondered what they are thinking? If you have at any time asked yourself any of those questions, you are not alone. The voyage down memory lane that we all take is usually filled with an inquisitive desire to gain an explanation about our past.

Like you, I used to think that every time a board of education met at my seat of learning it was because someone did not like me. Whether it was at home or at school, the boundaries of discipline never left me feeling better for the experience. In addition, I did not buy for a minute the awe-inspiring pronouncement that it was actually hurting the person doling out the punishment more than it was going to hurt me.

A blessing of this past week included one such disciplinarian who beckoned me to come to her home and partake of a meal. Three and a half decades after invoking fear in me, the gentleness of her hug, the warmth of her embrace, and the tearstained cheeks glowing with pride were a stark contrast to the taskmaster of yore. When the layers of advice that were given to a child were peeled back, the words of hope that came over an intercom every morning became real again.

It was from those early pictures painted for us in a small missionary school in India that the journey became possible. As I stood to make the speech on how to become effective as a global communicator in a world gone flat, I paused to pay homage to the headmistress of that school who was now wiping tears of joy as she watched one of the students she had guided become an expositor of her own messages. What a blessing to have been the recipient of that discipline.

The world has changed for both of us, and the path that culminated briefly in the foothills of East Tennessee was a reunion that was joyous. We reminisced about the stories of that southeastern Indian town and laughed at some of the pranks I had pulled and the reprimand that followed. We regaled each other with the glory that was teaching, and the teacher blessed the student who had now become a teacher. She was thanked by many that day for the role she had played and the influence she had wielded in shaping a life. The trademark sternness that was instilled in me as a child was now replaced with a brimming expression of validation as if to say, "Well done, my blessed child."

This week look for the blessings in your own life that came from the discipline of the past. Call the ones who disciplined you and thank them for loving you enough to correct you. Then make an effort to bring them into your present, if opportunity allows—and you will know exactly what I am saying.

A former student who is currently a leading doctor in the United Kingdom wrote a few weeks ago and said, "Thank you for believing in me when I did not."

Another former student who is a leading immigration lawyer often reminds me that every time I passed her classroom or entered the class to teach, she said to herself, "I want to be a strong woman like her."

Another. When he had dinner in our home, he told Sandy that one day over the intercom I had said, "Boys and girls, do not lose your integrity; there will be nothing left to live for." He is at present in a top position in the international banking world.

Former students are making a difference in the world, which makes me happy, proud, and grateful to God for the blessing of being a teacher. Their telephone calls, notes of gratitude, and love for the school and staff make me emotional.

Several of the former students are professors in reputed universities in India and abroad, including the United States. Some are owners of businesses, business executives, doctors, entrepreneurs, heads of educational institutions. One is retired from serving in the United Nations; another is a retired rear admiral of the Indian Navy; another is currently serving as rear admiral of the Southern Command; one is currently in charge of The National Institute of Virology, Pune, India. These attribute their success in life to their alma mater, Timpany School, Visakhapatnam. I thank God for their success and the dedicated team

Timpany Alumni Reunion in Knoxville on Mercy's 80th Birthday

of teachers and staff. You can never do this alone or single-handedly. To God be the glory, great things he does when we let him use us as instruments. Along with gratitude, there's always a question or two: Did I ever speak a discouraging word? Could I/we have done more? Regrets come late, and they often cannot be corrected.

The following verses were composed by former student Meenakshi Anantaram and read at the reunion of former students at Bangalore in 2009.

The Timpany School Mistress

Beside yon straggling fence that skirts the way
With blossom'd frutz unprofitably gay,
There, in her mansion, skill'd to rule
The Timpany Big Miss taught her little school.

A woman severe she was, and stern in view,
I knew her well, and every truant knew;
Well had the boding tremblers learn'd to trace
The day's disasters in her morning face.

Yet she was kind; or if severe in aught,
The love she bore to learning was in fault.
The school all declared how much she knew;
'Twas certain she could write, and cipher too:

Lands she could measure, terms and tides presage,
And e'en the story ran that she could gauge.
In arguing too, the person own'd his skill,
For e'en though vanquish'd she could argue still;

While worlds of learned length and thund'ring sound
Amazed the gazing rustics rang'd around;
And one small head could carry all she knew.

But past is all her fame. The very spot
Where many a time her triumph was forgot
As I go on.......

So let this morning a lesson to us be
To hold to our hearts the beautiful she
The one who molded us in her plan
And taught us to uphold the ideals of man!

She who brought us confidence to our life
And helped us on in all our strife
The time has come for us to bow down
And pray that no day for her is forlorn.

As life moves on in its colorful flow
O God, let at this moment Miss Jazz know
That 1000's of young hearts beat the rhythm of love
And are thankful for her...to the God above.

May her days ahead be strewn with peace
May the warmth of love keep her from disease
And when the time comes for her to move on
Let her know on that great dawn

That she rules our hearts and minds forever
We will never forget her...never ever!
For she is the hand that touched our space
And lifted us forever up in her grace.

O lovely one with the gentle face
This moment is for you and your noble race.

Part Three

Reflections

I can honestly say with the psalmist, "Surely your goodness and love will follow me all the days of my life" (Ps 23:6). The lessons life teaches are valuable. Joseph went from the pit and prison to having God exalt him and make him second in command in Pharaoh's court (Gen 41). Daniel came out of the den of lions unharmed (Dan 6). God was with them, and everyone knew God was with them.

It is easy to trust God when life is easy, but the true test is when we come out of fiery trials rock solid in our faith and trust in God. Those who do this are the "salt of the earth," who continue to bless everyone they meet. Humility is the hallmark and crown of glory of a successful leader.

Today I am more blessed than I ever was. I can identify with those who go through similar experiences. The concept that God punishes us according to our sins is not biblical. David prayed, "See if there is any offensive way in me, and lead me in the way everlasting" (Ps 139:24). Do not beat yourself up. We live in a world where values are warped and different theories and philosophies confuse us. We must stay focused on a loving God, who says, "Come to me, all you who are weary and burdened, and I will give you rest" (Matt 11:28).

It is not the wealth or power you have but the love you share that lifts the spirit of others. A smile, a cheery word, appreciation, encouragement will brighten the world. A friend of mine saw an elderly man gazing at the yogurt shelf in the grocery store and offered to help. He broke down and mentioned he had lost his wife for whom he picked up yogurt always. He thanked her for her concern. Love people, and do small acts of thoughtfulness—they will go a long way to encourage and comfort a lonely soul. Each day, find some way you can lift the burden of a lonely soul and bring comfort. Maya Angelou said, "Try to be a rainbow in someone's cloud."

On Being a Woman in a Man's World

In my case it was also being a single woman! The saying goes, "Behind every successful man is a woman." I would like to change this to *beside*. A woman need not be behind. She is beside and sometimes outruns a man. A single woman is never alone because God is with her. Women, married and single, have excelled in many fields. They nobly served in spite of many hurdles. Each one of us is original—your fingerprints are only yours. The results of your labor of love will speak for themselves, and they are your reward. Marian Wright Edelman once said, "If you don't like the way the world is, change it. You have an obligation to change it. You must do it, one step at a time…. Begin where you live and the ripples of change will expand…. When you cease to make a contribution, you begin to die."

I once read a notable quote: "The strength of a woman lies in being herself full of love, affection and beauty. She is the one that eventually makes a difference in the family and in society at large."

Did I face discrimination? Yes, I did. Did it hurt me? Yes! Did it make me less effective? The answer is an emphatic no! It is God and God's grace that sustained me. "I can do all this through [Christ] who gives me strength" (Phil 4:13). Most of the time, I did not retaliate and waste time and energy on those who hurt me. I had better things to do. Every woman should know of her strength. Eleanor Roosevelt said, "No one can make you feel inferior without your consent" and "A woman is like a tea bag: you will never know how strong it is until it's in hot water!" Let all the single women shout, "Let the water boil!" With God's help, we can "run through a troop."

When confronted with requests to show special favors for admission, word went around that such favors were not granted. "When Miss Jeyaraja Rao says, 'No,' she says it so politely that until we walked out of her office, we did not quite get it," said a high-ranking official in town. This saved me from pressure to oblige. There are no favored ones. Students could never boast that they were in school by virtue of their father's status. When a few parents came with a list of complaints about the school, they were usually the ones who did not keep up with the progress of their children. I listened, and the solution was simple.

I said, "I love your children and wish them the best in life. I will send them with my blessing. Here is the notepad. Apply for the transfer, and I will give it to you right now!" Invariably, their response was, "You know this is the best school in town." "Why, then, are we wasting time?" The word went around, and there were very few complaints thereafter!

There was much to learn. The first year as a teacher, I disciplined a boy who was bullying others. His mother complained to the manager, "A single woman cannot love children, and you must fire her." I was deeply hurt that the mother did not know that I loved children. The manager did not bring the matter up with me, but a teacher whispered what she heard. That night, I gave it some thought and felt the mother had a right to complain that a single woman cannot love children and prayed that I would have the heart of a mother like Deborah who was known as "a mother in Israel" (Judg 5). "More are the children of the desolate [unmarried?] woman than of her who has a husband" (Isa 54:1). A loving heart is God's special gift to every woman, single, married, or widowed. Single women have played a major role in the world with their accomplishments. They have been circumspect and modest and gained the respect of everyone. They have taken a stand for what is right and moral.

I cautiously chose the places I went or people with whom I associated. A girl in grade four wrote a composition on "What I want to be when I grow up." She mentioned that she wanted to be like Ms. J (this is what she called me) and added that she saw me coming from church on a Wednesday evening. Though I was not her teacher, I realized my life was under the microscope. I chose the places I went and avoided movies. We are trendsetters and role models, especially to children. If you are a single woman, never underestimate your worth and value or despise your singlehood! Mother Teresa said, "I alone cannot change the world, but I can cast a stone across the water to create ripples throughout world."

How did I face humiliation, insults, and rejection? God's promises in the Bible and Sandy's encouragement sustained me. For two years I struggled after the schools were taken over and often asked, "Why?" I spent long hours on my knees, praying. One day Sandy said, "Where is your faith? Trust God and let go." I looked back over God's faithfulness over the years and lay my burden at his feet. Peace flooded my soul. Jesus prayed when they crucified him, "Father, forgive them, for they do not know what they are doing" (Luke 23:34). I began to pray for those who caused this pain that God would bless them and that students in school would continue to learn true values. On a Wednesday,

I was at a Bible study led by a young attorney. He talked about reconciliation and quoted this verse. God spoke to my heart, and I mailed a letter blessing the person responsible for all this. It was the right thing—to walk the second mile. It was a closed chapter. I continue to enjoy the love and confidence of my colleagues and former students. Visits from them and letters remind me that my work was not in vain. Trials and rejection have made me strong. When you are a single woman in a man's world, you can survive by being tough and strong!

On Heroes, Sung and Unsung

During my travels around the world, I met some great men and women who have blessed the world with their service, wisdom, and life.

1. Anne Graham Lotz, Dr. Billy Graham's daughter, president and CEO of AnGel Ministries and author of several books, was the keynote speaker when BWA–WD met in Melbourne, Australia, January 2000, when I was the president. Her passion and deep commitment to people of the world spoke to our hearts.

2. President Corazon Aquino of Philippines and first female president of Asia. We visited her in the Malacanang Palace, Manila, and were impressed with her concern for young people. She requested the officers of BWA to emphasize the importance of faith and to instill its importance in their lives. She was a devout mother.

3. Archbishop Tutu of South Africa, Nobel Prize winner, educator, civil rights activist, and prominent spiritual leader, carried the spirit of grace, and his remarks reflected that there is no room for hatred.

4. Corrie ten Boom of Haarlem, Netherlands, was sent to a concentration camp and finally to death row and was miraculously saved. She and her family hid Jews in their home to protect them from concentration camps. We were in Lausanne, Switzerland, waiting to hear her. She walked in saying, "Children, do not wrestle but nestle in God's arms." There was not a dry eye when she shared of her experiences of torture and watching loved ones be killed. "Forgiveness is the key that unlocks the door of resentment and the handcuffs of hatred," she said.

5. Coretta King, wife of Dr. Martin Luther King Jr., kept her poise and faith after his assassination. Her courage to stand by her husband and her grace are special gifts.

6. Nannie Burrows, an educator, religious leader, and social activist of the National Baptist Women's Convention in the United States, carried the presence of Jesus. In 1960 a friend took me to see her. As she lay in bed, she radiated joy, and when she held my hand and prayed a prayer of blessing, I felt I was standing on holy ground.

7. Dr. Cynthia Perry Ray, a woman of passion and devotion, was president of the National Baptist Women's Convention of North America from 1995–2000. She invited me to bring the keynote address at its annual conference and told me I should be dressed in white. Sandy, who was the only white person in attendance, was dressed in a white sari and had a seat on the platform. Women dressed in white walked with the dancing and singing, waving their convention banner: "When the saints go marching in, Lord, I want to be in that number, when the saints go marching in." While I delivered the message, the dear women shouted, "Hallelujah! Preach on, sister! Glory, hallelujah! Amen, sister!" It did not distract me; in fact, Sandy said I swayed to their shouts! The joy and fervor of the dear women was infectious indeed! I had a similar experience at Judson College in Alabama when I received an honorary doctorate of ministry.

8. I met Bilawal Bhutto Zardari, son of Prime Minister Benazir Bhutto of Pakistan, at the National Prayer Breakfast 2010 in Washington, DC. I blessed him to be strong and brave. I told him that we stood in silence and prayed for the Bhutto family and people of Pakistan at the morning assembly at school when we heard of his grandfather's death. Some asked me if it was appropriate to do this because of the strained relationship between the two countries. I reasoned that for a great leader, a father, husband, and grandfather, all differences should be set aside, especially in times of sorrow. Students should not get involved in politics since half-knowledge and poor knowledge are dangerous.

9. In 1958 I met Mrs. George Martin, president of BWA–WD in Calcutta, and was blessed by her vision for the women of the world, especially for Asian women. In Rio 1960, I met two great women, Mrs. Marie Mathis and Miss Alma Hunt. For several of us from Asia, it was an awesome experience to sit most nights in Mrs. Mathis's room to share our stories and be encouraged as she lovingly broadened our vision for the women of the world. Miss Hunt made us laugh with her many jokes! Others who challenged us to look beyond ourselves and serve the women of the world are Dr. Marion Bates, dean of women, McMaster University, Hamilton, ON, Canada, and president of BWA–WD, 1960–1965; Mrs. C. W. Dengate, first executive secretary of the Baptist Women's Missionary Society; Mrs. Catherine Allen, president of BWA–WD, 1985–1990; Mrs. Audrey Morikawa, president of BWA–WD, 2000–2005.

10. The greatest of all experiences was to stand before Mother Teresa as she walked into the waiting room in Nirmal Hirday (Home of the Pure Heart), Calcutta. There she stood with folded hands, radiating the presence of Jesus. She had come from her worship time and was leaving to walk the streets of Calcutta, to touch, love, and serve the poor and dying. Her famous words have blessed the world: "I see Christ in the dying." The movie *Letters* is about her and her consuming love for people who were not hers and her desire to bring comfort and solace to the hurting. She put feet to her prayers and went out into a hurting world.

The unknown, unsung heroes all over the world who silently but lovingly blessed my life make the world a better place for everyone. Some of them walked miles to conventions and sold snacks to cover travel expenses. Back home, they met in groups under trees to worship God, saving their meager rations for visitors. Women brought handmade crafts to sell at conferences and turned in the money, most of the time, to pay convention expenses. In an Indian village hundreds of women gathered for four days. They saved a handful of rice and dhal (lintel), which they pooled, and each meal was tasty with the love and sacrifice that went into it. Their names never hit headlines except in the annals of heaven. I mentioned earlier the elderly man in Rio who prayed for India for thirteen years, not knowing where it was. These are unnamed saints who, in the quiet of their humble homes, pray for their town, their country, and the world and may never see the results. Mary Hutson, a godly woman, saw me in 1960 when I was in Little Rock, Arkansas, and prayed for me for thirty-five years. The result of her prayers was my going to Buenos Aires in 1995, and the rest is history.

Was life a bed of roses to any of these women? Certainly not. However, in spite of their struggles, they made the world a better place for us. The battles they fought and victories they won have left us with a challenge and a legacy. What is our legacy to the next generation?

On Life with Children: Lessons Learned

"Jesus loves the little children, all the children of the world. Red and yellow, black and white, all are precious in his sight. Jesus loves the little children of the world." This was a favorite chorus in school. We had all shades of color in school, and they formed a beautiful mosaic. When children held hands and sang "We Are the World," the audience and staff watched them with misty eyes. Adults can discriminate, but children do not.

My niece sent me a bookmark with a picture of her son, Sammy, which read, "A hundred years from now, the world may be different because I was important in the life of a child." Let us make sure we are important in the life of every child.

Children grow to be what they see and hear, especially at home. Words and actions either build or break their lives. At the funeral of a couple who died in a car crash, their young boy wanted the gathering to sing "You Are My Sunshine," his favorite chorus, which his mom sang to him every morning. "This Little Light of Mine" was another favorite. Make beautiful memories for your children, as sweet memories will help ease their sorrow and loss. Pray, kiss, and send them with your blessing whenever you leave home. What happens at home leaves indelible memories of joy or pain.

A teacher once brought a girl to my office, as she was not doing her work and kept asking to telephone her mother. She was jittery, but as she sat in my office, she calmed down. When I asked why she wanted to call her mother, her response was that the previous night her parents had had an argument and her mother had threatened that she would return to her parents the next day. I allowed her to call her mother, and after the call she looked happy and returned to class. I remember a story of a little boy who got hurt on his way to school by a bus. The doctor asked, "Son, did you not hear the bus?" The boy said that morning before he left for school, the owner of their apartment told his mom that she would be evicted by evening if she did not pay her dues and she was crying. "Her crying was loud in my ears, and I did not hear the bus." Are there some valuable lessons to remember?

What is clear to us may not necessarily mean the same to children. During the lunch break, I heard a lot of running and shouting in some classrooms. I turned on the intercom and said, "I am sick and tired of your behavior." I gave the kids a good talking-to and shortened their free time on the field. When they returned to their rooms in absolute silence, I continued the talk! I was banging on the keys of my typewriter to let out steam. I saw the white head of a kindergarten boy at the door of my office. He would not leave though I told him thrice to return to class and take his nap. He walked up to me with a concerned look, tapped my hand, and asked, "Principal, are you sick and tired?" When I said, "No," he pointed to the intercom and said, "You said you are sick." I hated myself that my anger brought out the best in this child. I hugged him and told him I was fine and to go back to class. When I came out of the washroom after a good cry, he looked at my eyes and said, "Yes, you are sick." I told him I was not and led him to the class. He stopped by the office and told the girls, "Take care of the principal. She is sick." That evening, his mother called to see if I was still sick! This happened in 1968, and I have not once uttered these words! I prayed every day that I would not hurt or cause confusion in a child.

Children absorb everything we say and do. We once met two little girls with their parents in a restaurant. They chatted with us, and as they were leaving, one of them said, "Men are nothing but trouble. Stay away from them." The father smiled. Where did they hear this? We had another boy who continued to have nightmares later in life because he still hears his parents quarrelling at night. Angry parents, beware. Children are good imitators, and we have a solemn responsibility to mold them with love and care.

A friend of mine was washing clothes, and her little son kept troubling her. She lost her cool and said, "Stop it or Jesus will punish you." A few minutes later she saw him standing before the picture of Jesus with folded hands, praying, "Jesus, do not punish me. I will wash all your dirty clothes." She thought it was a joke. Our words and actions should not give a wrong concept of God. Children are paying attention, and we should be careful about what we do.

Duncan was very good at sports. He participated in an interschool sports meet, and when he returned, he was crying because the umpire had bypassed him and announced the one who came behind him as the winner. I told him, "Duncan, it is fine. Calm down. God knows the truth. You will win next time." It pierced my heart when he said, "God did not do this. That man did it." Adults are under scrutiny/surveillance. Children's little ears hear, and their eyes see when we least expect that they are absorbing what we say and do. At the assembly, the little ones are often asked to sing, "Oh, be careful, little ears, what you hear…little eyes what you see…little tongue what you speak."

Children are compassionate and sensitive to those in need and pain. On Sundays, some of us met to pray for our town. One of them brought her little sister, Marjorie. She decided to pray a sweet, heartfelt short prayer and ended, "Jesus, bless all the 'cracked people' on the main road." Though we were tickled and smiled, she taught us a valuable lesson to be compassionate to the less fortunate. Do we ever pray for the homeless or lonely? God does answer prayer.

My sister cried a lot after her husband died. Her little granddaughter Suzy took her to the bird cage in her home and said, "Granny, this bird is still singing. Her husband died. Don't cry."

One day she took me to the living room where my mom was watching a movie of Jesus's crucifixion. She begged me, "Don't let those men kill Jesus. Come, do something to stop them." I had seen the same movie before but did not have the same reaction. Am I sensitive to what it cost Jesus to redeem me?

Suzy is the one who once told me not to make her teacher cry when I spoke at the morning assembly. The young teacher had lost her husband suddenly from a massive heart attack. Later, the teacher told me that Suzy stood next to her teacher every morning when she saw her tears.

At home, we were discussing Christian N. Barnard, the South African surgeon who performed the world's first human-to-human heart transplant. My little nephew David asked my sister what it was about and then asked her if Jesus was in that heart. My sister came to ask what she should tell him, and when she got back, he was kneeling, asking Jesus to come into that heart! Be prepared to answer the questions children ask, and be sensitive.

Duncan was a third-grader, and I taught Bible. I told the class that God created Adam and Eve and he came to them in the garden of Eden "in the cool of the evening." When I reviewed the lesson the following week, I asked why God created them and why he came to the garden. Duncan answered, "God is soooo lonely. He wanted to talk to them, and I think he wants to talk to us." It is a profound truth.

Children are fragile, and woe to those who cause sorrow to them. A brother and sister were in grades one and two and lost their loving mother. They came late to school one day and refused to go home in the evening. The teacher brought them to me, and while I was talking to her, I saw a former schoolmate of mine slap the little girl. She was an angry stepmother. According to her, they walked out of the house the previous evening. It was heartbreaking to see the girl with folded hands sobbing and begging to be forgiven, saying she would never do that again. She got another slap. This was at least forty years ago, and I still pray for them. I saw the anger of a stepmother and continue to struggle at the thought of children who face a similar situation. "Can a mother forget the baby at her breast and have no compassion on the child she has borne? Though she may forget, I will not forget you!" (Isa 49:15). Mothers need to love the children God entrusts to them.

It does not take much to feel loved. To make children feel loved is a sacred trust, and a teacher can play many roles. Children should know there is a lot of love in the heart of the one who disciplines them. At school we always prayed at a special assembly for children who had a death in the family. Almost twenty-five years later, one student wrote to me that he wished he were still in school to hear the whole school pray for him and his family as his father had just died! Another student lost his mother in a tragic accident. When I visited his home, he gave me a smile that brought tears to my eyes. After he graduated from school, he brought me his wedding invitation, and said, "Come to my wedding and take my mother's place." I traveled to another state and had a seat where I could see the ceremony, and he kept looking at me during the ceremony. The mother of a first-grader passed away in childbirth, and I went to view her body, and he ran up to me just for a hug. I made sure to attend students' weddings and visited their home when there was a death. It bonded me to my precious children. I always reminded them that my intent to hold the bar high was because I loved them so they would achieve great heights of success in the world.

Children do have deep feelings, too, so one should never say, "You do not understand." They do understand and comprehend more than we think.

Never discipline a child in public. It humiliates a child. Discipline a child, taking him aside because he did wrong, not because he made you angry or embarrassed you. Be sure to hug your child and pray. Never, ever say, "Can't you do anything right?" "You will never amount to anything?" Really? How do you know? Did someone say this to you, and do you recall how it made you lack self-esteem?

On Old Age

It catches up with us before we know we are there! Every day is a gift and bonus. Learn to grow old gracefully. When the time came to use a cane and go for weekly therapy, I had to swallow my pride. A tree stops growing, flowers fade, and lions lose their sharp claws. This is true of the human body. Strength gives way to weakness. Gone are the days when I ran more than walked and was quite an athlete. My children reading this will smile! All of us have to climb the ladder of old age steadily, as there is no way to climb down! We must keep our mind active and memory sharp. At the meeting of the local Rotary Club when I was invited to speak, the president, while introducing me, said, "Women get up to forty and thereafter stay there." Really? Yes, I am grateful for my age and proud of every wrinkle I have earned! Age makes you wise, content, cautious in thought, word, and behavior. Life is lived leisurely, and there is time to appreciate nature and stand and stare. Age teaches you not to be rash and not be an authority on every subject. Opinions expressed unasked make one look foolish. Polonius, in Shakespeare's *Hamlet*, says, "Give thy thoughts no tongue.... Give every man thy ear, but few thy voice.... To thine own self be true" (I.3). Do not judge anyone. Jesus said, "Do not judge, and you will not be judged" (Luke 6:37). My dad always reminded us that when we point a finger to judge others, four fingers are pointing back to us. In fact, when we judge others, two things happen: Our remarks are either ignored or people make note of our own faults and keep their distance from us lest we do the same to them! So why ask for trouble? Just pray for that individual.

Remember not to say, "Gone are the golden days. Life was wonderful in the past." Let us ask, "What difference did I make to make it better?" In our younger days we smiled when we heard the elderly say this and we wondered what they were saying. But are we saying the same thing?

The days of the rat race are behind me. My life is lived leisurely and stress-free, and I have earned the right to relax and set my own pace. When I was young, working and traveling, I wondered if there would ever be a time when I could get up when I wanted to and enjoy leisure time. Complaining makes one sour, and people shun us, whereas a smile draws them to you.

The choice is ours: to complain or accept old age as part of life. Dwelling on the past does not get us anywhere. We can accept who we are today and limit our activities to what we can do. The past is behind, so we can make every day beautiful for ourselves and others. We can radiate love and have a zest for life. If we count our blessings, we may be surprised that they outweigh our hurts. Continue to pray for those who hurt you. All of us carry scars of betrayal. But we can avoid mulling on them and engaging in self-pity. We can do unto others what we want them to do for us. If we thrive on negativity, it will make us miserable and we are the loser.

My grandmother often told us that nothing is right to a person who finds fault with others: how others sit, stand, talk, and smile. We should beware of the know-it-all person, as we may be the next target. Life is too short to waste one's time judging others. We should take time to meditate and pray. "Finally, brothers and sisters, whatever is true, whatever is noble, whatever is right, whatever is pure, whatever is lovely, whatever is admirable—if anything is excellent or praiseworthy—think about such things" (Phil 4:8). A happy person with a positive outlook has many friends. Complaining people are loners and cannot be trusted. I am grateful for each day that I am alive. I can see, hear, smell, eat, and enjoy creation; I can walk, shower, and communicate. God's blessings are many, and as you keep counting them, there is no time for complaints.

"I was young and now I am old, yet I have never seen the righteous forsaken or their children begging bread" (Ps 37:25). "Your strength will equal your days" (Deut 33:25). "Even to your old age and gray hairs I am he, I am he who will sustain you. I have made you and I will carry you; I will sustain you and I will rescue you" (Isa 46:4). "Sow your seed in the morning, and at evening let your hands not be idle, for you do not know which will succeed, whether this or that, or whether both will do equally well" (Eccl 11:6).

Never think life is over and no good thing will happen to you. Stop and name the things you can do and admire; jot down helpful thoughts that cross your mind; admire God's creation and the manifestation of his power in the sunrise, sunset, clouds, moon, and stars.

Anna was an eighty-year-old prophetess who was praying in the temple and saw baby Jesus when he was brought by his parents (Luke 2:36–38). Simeon (God-receiver) was told by the Holy Spirit that he would not die until he had seen the Lord Christ, and when he held baby Jesus in the temple, he prayed, *Nunc dimittis*, and prophesied Jesus's crucifixion. Simeon was then ready to die (Luke 2:25–35). Elizabeth, an elderly woman, was a friend to a teenager, Mary. Elizabeth told Mary, "No word from God will ever fail" (Luke 2:37). Age should not deter us from having a smile, a twinkle, and a kind word. Bless those whom you meet, and be a friend to young people. Age does not preclude you from being a blessing to others, both young and old. As you get older, you will understand more and more that it's not about what you look like or what you own. It's all about the person you've become.

Message to the Elderly

I am ninety years old. I have experienced joy, sorrow, pain, and rejection. My message to you is this: It takes a lot of chiseling for a rock to become a piece of beautiful sculpture. In the fiery furnace of affliction, the dross in our lives is refined. Share your successes and failures with the young who seek your counsel, and write the story of your life. It may help others. Follow your heart, and use your God-given gifts. They are yours not by accident.

You are as old as you think you are. Often say, "The best is yet to come." Say a cheery word. Bless everyone you meet, and remember to say, "God bless you." You will never know if they have given up hope. Be lavish in commending and appreciating when deserved. Be polite. Your life of contentment and joy is infectious. Pray as you pass by places of worship, schools, workers in shops, and those who come to your mind. You may never know the needs of people, but God does. The world around us is in need. Take time to pray for the world with an atlas open. You will recall the elderly man in Rio de Janeiro who prayed for India for thirteen years. We may never see the results of our prayers, but eternity will. At a Mexican restaurant a young server greets everyone, saying, "Every day is a good day." At a Burger King drive-thru the woman said as she handed the bag out the window, "Have the greatest day." She was tired but looked beyond herself to cheer the customer. How do we respond? Smile and say a silent prayer. Prayers are not always for big issues but for simple ones.

Do not throw or attend a pity party. Self-pity kills your joy and the joy of those you meet. Eat healthily and exercise. Never be too busy. Follow your intuitions: call, pray, send a note to one who is lonely or facing difficult circumstances. Do not pry into their problems, and do not divulge confidences. You are at an age when many things have changed. Customs and dress have changed because the world has shrunk and our view of the world has widened. Listen to your body, and do not stretch your strength on unimportant matters. Age does not entitle you to judge others. Remove the beam in your eye first (Matt 7:1). Your remarks can discourage a weak soul instead of building their faith in God, in humanity, and in themselves. Dad once told us that a mother had cleaned the French window thoroughly and when her little girl returned from school, she told her the view is clear. The child said, "Mom, there is a spot there. You did not clean it." Are we guilty of thoughtless remarks?

Message to Parents

Do I see a smile on your face and hear you say, "What do you know?"

Children are a gift from God. You hold the future in your hands. Encourage them to achieve their dream through hard work, honesty, and excellence.

As much as you love your children, parents should be wise. Teach your children early that privileges are not an entitlement; they are earned, and parents are not a bank from which children can draw. Children should never be a burden. They should save a portion of their salary or the allowance you give to them. Later, this habit will keep them from buying things they cannot afford and from getting into debt. When they are on their own, they will be grateful to you for the lessons you inculcated in them.

The family is a beautiful unit. Spend time together and your children will follow your example. We live in a busy world. Family and home play an important role in the behavior of your children.

Our strength is in our diversity. Hold on to one thing: Love people. Love children for who they are, and respect them. Children cannot choose their family or status in life.

Never be too busy, and never tell your children, "I am busy. Do not disturb me." Sitting together for breakfast and dinner as a family has great value when everyone shares the happenings of the day. I recently heard of a mother who tells her family that before they come to dinner, they must leave their cell phones in a basket that is in the hallway.

Never compare your children to their siblings. Each one is unique; assure them of your love for them just as they are. You are their role model. Be present and interested in your child's day-to-day life. Share their joys and fears, and answer their questions. I have heard some children complain, "My dad is working for others, and he has no time for me." Lost time never can return. Invest time, money, and love in your child. God has entrusted them to you, and you play a major role in shaping their character. Their wings grow fast, and they fly away. What draws them to you are the sweet memories you have made. Children crave your love that gifts and money cannot replace. The old saying that "a family that prays together stays together" is true. Your love for each other will be an example when they have families of their own. I heard of an elderly husband who left a love note for his wife before he left for work every morning!

The world is a better place because of good people like these. Plant a kiss on your child before you leave. This goes a long way in a child's day and life.

A mother once complained that her older son was disobedient and gave her a lot of trouble. I sat with him in my office, and as we chatted, he complained that his mother favors his younger brother and does not like him. I remembered his mother had told me that the younger boy had seizures and needed attention. When I told him that his brother has some health issues, he was surprised, cried, and said he did not know about it. He apologized to his mother that evening and hugged his brother. If the mother had explained this to him, there would have been no strained feelings and no problem. Do not expect a child to understand what may be clear to you. Talk to your children in love, and they will share their fears and failures. Admonish them when they are wrong and tell them the consequences of bad decisions. Think long and hard with your words and actions, as they leave marks and scars on a child's sensitive heart. Children love their parents and crave their love. On a sweeter note: A friend told us that one night the family gathered for prayer and her little son asked his mom to pray for his teacher. She told him to pray for her. He did and ended his prayer, "God, you are the best." Have we ever told/thanked God for his love because he is the best?

Message to the Younger Generation

Children should be grateful to their parents, grandparents, and the elderly. Children are here because of them. They took care of us in sickness, in health, in joy, and in sorrow. They made sacrifices to give us what they did not have. Are we grateful? Never ignore them. We are preoccupied with ourselves and forget that we will one day be in their place. The needs of the older generation are few and simple. All they want is love, a telephone call, greetings on special days, and a note that reads, "I love you." If they live with you, include them in your conversation and at mealtimes. They do ask questions as their world has shrunk, contact with it is limited, and they need a little information. Do not say, "It does not concern you," and do not ignore their presence. "Honor your father and your mother, so that you may live long in the land the LORD your God is giving you" (Exod 20:12), the only commandment with a promise.

While Jesus was on the cross, he entrusted his mother to John, the beloved disciple: "When Jesus saw his mother there, and the disciple whom he loved standing nearby, he said to her, 'Woman, here is your son,' and to the disciple, 'Here is your mother.' From that time on, this disciple took her into his home" (John 19:26–27). Do not draw on your parents' resources. It is your responsibility to keep them living in comfort. Some day you will be in their position. It does not take much to make parents and older people happy. Little acts of love and thoughtfulness are all they need.

When my three nephews call me, their first words are distinct and bring me joy. The eldest: "Are you busy? Is it a good time to call you, Auntie?" The second: "Auntie, are you okay? Sorry I did not call you in a while." The third: "Auntie, uh…how are you?" Their greetings are special and precious. Their wives and their children have a special way when they call. Just as an aunt is thrilled to hear her family's voices, God is happy to hear us calling him "Father God"! On resurrection morning Mary Magdalene, stricken with grief, stood at the empty tomb. She saw a figure and thought he was the gardener and asked if he knew where her master was. She heard Jesus call her name, "Mary," and her response was "Rabboni" (Master!). Yes, there is a characteristic way God, family, and friends call us. It is a comforting voice when God calls our name. "But now, this is what the LORD says—he who created you, Jacob [substitute your name]…. 'Do not fear, for I have redeemed you; I have summoned you by name; you are mine'" (Isa 43:1).

Never forget the father and mother who brought you into this world. Their love is precious. There was a plane crash in a city in India, and everyone was dead. They found the charred body of a mother with her infant in her arms. This is a mother's love. Some children may have parents who never experienced love of a father or mother. They should not treat their own children in a similar way. You have the choice to break "the generational sin."

I was visiting a family in a particular city in the United States in 1960, and a mother shared that their son had walked out of their home and they were heart-broken. We prayed together, and the next day they invited their son to meet me. He was in the service where I brought the message. She prepared a special meal that her son liked, and the sisters bought an ice cream cake that he liked. After lunch we sat in the living room, read a passage of Scripture, and prayed. There was silence until the father got up and said, "Son, since you left us, we have kept your room and bed ready waiting for you to return. Come home!" Son and father embraced, and I heard that he returned home. The parable of the prodigal son came alive. Another friend of mine had a son who came home late at night. She sat in the living room praying. One night when she heard his scooter, she turned on the front lights, and the young man saw a snake coiled on the gate. A mother's love and prayers saved him from a poisonous snake! The love of parents is unmatched.

Many years ago, I read of a mother's love for her wavering son who left home years ago. One day he returned home and went to his bedroom and found bis bed neatly made with a note and a red rosebud on the bedside table. The note said, "My son, every day since you left, I have written a note and a put a fresh rose in the vase, hoping and praying you would return. I love you and pray for you." The young man ran to her bedroom and found her dead. That's the love of a mother/father. It was too late for the son to undo what should have been done much earlier.

One evening we were having tea while my nephews were playing in the yard. They were laughing and talking aloud, and my sister got up and said, "Dave is crying." We told her that the boys were enjoying themselves. She ran out, and Dave had fallen and hurt himself. Only a mother can recognize her son's voice in a multitude of voices. Mothers, especially, make sacrifices for their families. Some of them prepare a good meal with the meager money an alcoholic husband brings home. She feeds him and the children and eats the leftovers. Do you recall when you returned home after being away that your Mom prepared dishes you like? Children, be grateful to them. You owe your parents love and gratitude. In the Indian culture, the eldest son takes care of his widowed mother.

My grandmother often cried about her unmarried and wavering son and asked my mom to sing, "Where is my wand'ring boy tonight? / The boy of my tend'rest care, / The boy that once was my joy and light, / The child of my love and pray'r / Oh, where is my boy tonight? / My heart o'er flows for I love him he knows, / Oh, where is my boy tonight?" Only a mother can love her wavering children and her arms are ready to embrace and welcome them home.

It was always after dinner on a Friday night that the members of Timpany School Society met with a very long agenda. Every member was tired after a week of hard work. I got home after midnight, and my mother was waiting for me in the living room. When I asked her why she was not sleeping, her answer was, "I cannot until I see you back home."

Do you recall the times when your mom waited for you to come home and she warmed the food and watched you as you ate? Do special memories of her make you stop and thank her, hug and kiss her? Do we take our loved ones for granted and forget all that they did not because they owed it to you but out of sheer love?

My second nephew lived next to our home, and every night my mother would tell me to call and find out if the children were all home. If I told her that their car was in and they were all safe and back home, it did not satisfy her until I called and confirmed. That is the love of a mother/grandmother!

Children and grandchildren, repay that love with little acts of thoughtfulness. Thank them often for cooking your favorite dishes, and relive the sweet memories they have made for you.

In Conclusion

Every stage of life teaches us many valuable lessons, and adventure is one of them. There is much yet to learn, to read, observe, and research. Take time to admire the world around you, which is God's creation. Keep your mind active. Life does not end until you take your last breath. The poet Walter de la Mare said, "What is this life if full of care? You have not time to stand and stare…. A poor life this, if full of care, we have no time to stand and stare."

The psalmist describes God's creation in Psalm 19. He saw God's handiwork and praised the Creator. Take time to admire the beauty of nature, and thank the Creator for making a beautiful and wonderful world for us to enjoy and preserve!

The three main stages of life:
1. The past: It is behind us and cannot be undone.
2. The present: Avoid the mistakes of the past, and let them not define who you are. Live every day to the fullest. Do not linger on the past.
3. The future: Do not fear it; rather, face it with faith in God and with hope (see 1 Tim 1:7). God will never leave you; let trust and love play a major role. Expect adventures every day. Corrie ten Boom said, "Never be afraid to trust an unknown future to a known God. God takes all our sins—the past, present, and future—and dumps them in the sea and puts up a sign that says 'No fishing allowed.'"

The game of life has rules and boundaries too. Stick to them. There are no shortcuts to real success. It requires discipline, integrity, and hard work. Do not shirk from hard work; it makes or breaks your career.

Be an encourager. Some parents are never satisfied with the performance of their children. Children are discouraged by remarks such as these: "An 'A' is not good. Get an 'A+.'" When it is an A+, never say, "Keep it up!" Commend the child. How would you feel if someone said this to you? Be an encourager all the time, and build their confidence. We are all simple, ordinary people who serve an extraordinary God who promises never to leave us. Never push open a closed door; enter the open door and achieve the unachievable. Instill this in children. There is pride when you are willing to do whatever it takes to make a difference in the world. A classic example is Booker T Washington. He was poor, yet that did not deter him from doing his best. Every job he was given was done to perfection. He was the founder of Tuskegee Institute in Alabama. How did he achieve this? It was not wealth or power but work done with integrity that made the difference. He said, "Nothing can come to one that is worth having, except as a result of hard work" and "Character, not circumstances, makes the man."

Do not be afraid to travel "the road not taken." Before us are two paths: One is safe since everyone chooses a well-worn, trusted path that results in success. The other is an unknown. It takes courage and adventure to choose the unknown road. Trust in God. Put feet and hands to your dreams, and you will be an achiever. We are the beneficiaries of the good deeds of others who dreamed big and did the impossible. Is there something we can achieve that will bless the next generation? These words should help us to be people of good repute: "Love all, trust a few, do wrong to none" (William Shakespeare, *All's Well That Ends Well*); "The fool doth think he is wise, but the wise knows himself to be a fool" (Shakespeare, *As You Like It*).

Love does not keep records of wrongs done. Keep short accounts. A judging spirit ruins your joy and usefulness. Every experience, whether of sorrow or joy, is a component that has made you who you are today. What are the memories you wish to leave? "The name of the righteous is used in blessings, but the name of the wicked will rot" (Prov 10:7). First, ask, "What if they are right and I am wrong?" What would you have done under similar circumstance? Do not let regrets and missed opportunities consume you. Acknowledge them and use them as lessons. Believe in yourself, and trust God for the present and future.

Share your happy experiences and God's goodness to you. How do we cope with sorrow, success, failure, unbelief, and loss? These are part of one's life. Do you know anyone who has not faced pain, loss, and sorrow? Share the benefits of clean and simple living, especially with the young. My pastor in India once told us there is no way we can count our blessings "one by one," as they are too many, and to count them "ton by ton." Take a few minutes every day and thank God for bringing you this far. Live each day as if it is your last. What are we grateful for? We visited an aunt of mine, and when she walked in to greet us, she said, "Sorry, I was having my shower. I thank God always for water!" I thought it was strange, but now I am grateful for things I used to take for granted. When someone thanks you for something you have done for them, it makes you happy. Gratitude is a lovely quality to cherish.

Beware of the sin of jealousy. Play the role God called you to, and carry a team with you. Together we succeed; alone we fail. Jealousy was the cause of the first murder. Cain resented that God was pleased with Abel's sacrifice and murdered him and tried to cover it. When God asked him where Abel was, his response was, "Am I my brother's keeper?" God replied, "Your brother's blood cries out to me from the ground" (Gen 4:9b, 10).

"Be sure that your sin will find you out" (Num 32:23). We can never lie to God, can we? Are there consequences when we lie to people? One of the dangers we face in life is jealousy when others have what you do not. Miriam, who loved her brother Moses, grew jealous of him and questioned his leadership (Num 12). Jealousy is a canker worm and eats away the best in us. Haman hung from the same gallows he built for Mordecai. "No one from the east or the west, or from the desert can exalt themselves. It is God who judges: He brings one down, he exalts another" (Ps 75:6–7). "I have learned to be content whatever the circumstances" (Phil 4:11).

Have time for people who come to you for advice to share their problems. Listen. Think. Draw from your own experiences, and keep their confidences. Wisdom is the hallmark of age. People ask, "How do you know that it is God speaking to you?" This is an understandable question as we live in a world that is always in a hurry and noisy. We must take a little time each day to get still before God, to focus on him, to shut out all thoughts, to listen to the "still small voice."

The hymn writer was right when he penned these lines, "I come to the garden alone, while the dew is still on the roses. And the voice I hear, falling on my ear, the Son of God discloses. And he walks with me, and he talks with me. And he tells me I am his own. And the joy we share as we tarry there, none other has ever known."

He meets us at the point of our need. You come away from your quiet time refreshed and strong. God's voice becomes familiar, as it is loving, never condemnatory or harsh, but tender. He picks us up at the point of our need and leads us "through green pastures and beside still waters" (Ps 23). Slow down the pace of your life. "Slow and steady wins the race" is a good rule to accept.

Pray especially for the less fortunate and those who are struggling with addictions. I once spoke to the patients in a lepers' hospital in my home state. As they walked into the meeting place, I smelled an odor that was not pleasant. They clapped their palms (they had no fingers) and sang praises to God. No handicap can stifle us from praising God.

Pray for compassion. I will never forget when Sandy and I went to the maximum security women's prison to share God's message. Our friend, Sharon Pallone, of Rose Bud, Arkansas, had a great ministry for decades with these women. She obtained the clearance for our visit. We went through multiple gates, waiting at each gate until we got the clearance to proceed. Little did we know what to expect. Young people from a local church were singing, and the music was turned to full blast: "When the saints came marching in, Lord, I want to be in that number, when the saints came marching in." Women walked in dressed in white, entered the hall clapping and singing. We remembered what John Bunyan said when he saw a man being led to the gallows: "There, but for the grace of God, goes John Bunyan."

Jesus chose twelve disciples who lived with him for three years, and he trained them to work as a team. Judas, one of the twelve, betrayed Jesus for thirty pieces of silver and later took his own life (Matt 26:15). Peter repented after he denied Jesus three times, and the resurrected Jesus entrusted to him his work. Three times he asked, "Peter, do you love me? Feed my sheep" (John 21:15–17). Peter preached the first sermon in the upper room. It was the beginning of the Christian church (Acts 2). For more than 2,000 years the church faced unimaginable persecution, but nothing has been able to destroy her. Be an encourager, and disciple those who are entrusted to you. Long after you are gone, the fruit of your labor of love will bless and build lives and let the "beat go on."

Kings and kingdoms rise and fall, but God's kingdom remains strong, and his message continues to change lives, heal the wounds of the brokenhearted, breathe peace into restless and troubled hearts, and answer our questions. This is the wonder of the message of Jesus because eleven disciples spread it in the then-known world. Lives continue to be changed, to prove Jesus' message is the answer to the world's problems.

Spiritual Reflections

God's plans for our lives are unfathomable. Make the best of your present, and he will take care of the rest. I pray that I will finish well and be faithful to my Lord until I take my last breath. If God had not redeemed me or if he takes his hand off of me, I am mere clay. What he has done for me, he can do for you. Trust him, and experience his faithfulness every day of your life.

Life has been exciting working with children and women of the world. I look forward each morning for something exciting to happen, and I am never disappointed. God's Word, a hymn, a happy memory, a note to someone lifts my spirit. I enjoy every moment and am content and happy. Sandy gives me more than I need. Life is restful, and days are peaceful. "Those who hope in the LORD will renew their strength. They will soar on wings like eagles; they will run and not grow weary, they will walk and not be faint" (Isa 40:31). God is faithful, and together we will run the race.

What did I learn visiting every continent of the world? I have learned not to thrive on praise and approval of people. I have learned to never resent constructive criticism. There is always room for improvement. I constantly remind myself that I am a learner and pray that I would not offend people of different cultures and customs. It is not my business to criticize or change the cultures of others. My passion is to share God's love for everyone and what God has done for me. I take care not to criticize or condemn, as those create distance. I try to be who I am and let others be who they are. I try to share what God has done in my life and the blessing of walking with him. Before traveling to Eastern Europe, well-meaning people advised me not to wear any jewelry, except my wedding ring (the only thing I never owned!), or bright-colored clothes. As I was traveling extensively, I did not press my clothes and wore a magenta sari, the only one left. When I stood up to speak, an elderly woman stood up and spoke loudly with gestures. I thought I had offended the dear woman until my translator said that the women love bright colors and wondered why I did not wear more of them. The women stood and clapped! Why do we misunderstand or judge people of different cultures?

I had mentioned earlier that one year at the Christmas program, children were dressed in the typical costume of the region they represented, locked hands, and sang "We Are the World." There was not a dry eye in a gathering of about 2,000 people.

Will those who come after we are gone sing this because we made the stones into bread and we reached out to the needy and lost? Let us make memories that will inspire others. May God help us leave the world better than we found it. Remove the tinted glasses and see that we are more alike than different. Take the first step toward the doubting and fearful with a smile and stretch out a helping hand. Long after you're gone, the deed will continue to bless others. Never look down upon those who do not look, dress, or speak like you! Be interested in people; share their pain and sorrow. The hymn "Rescue the Perishing, Care for the Dying" says, "Down in the human heart, crushed by the tempter / Feelings lie buried that grace can restore / Touched by a loving hand, wakened by kindness, / Chords that are broken will vibrate again." Everyone we meet is a human being with a soul and feelings like every one of us. Treat each person with dignity. We need to forget our egos and learn from others. Together, we form a beautiful mosaic. Your love for others will be like ripples and will bless many.

My greatest joy was to be in the presence of women who were struggling with deep scars of poverty, persecution, death of loved ones, holding malnourished infants but still smiling because of their faith in God. They have blessed me and made me a better person after meeting them and listening to their life stories. I went to them as a learner and not as a learned! Are there times when you are not grateful for your comforts and envy those who have more? Walk in the shoes of the needy and sick. Sometimes I have had parents of students in my school who were poor and studied under the streetlights and are now holding high positions. Their one desire was that their children should receive a good education. A few who had no opportunity to study wanted their children to have what they could not afford. One of our support staff had his two children in the school, and one is a doctor and the other is in the medical field. Two children who were students of the school are teaching English in Nepal. They came to school at night to study under the lights.

Do we judge others without knowing the circumstances that reflect what they say and do? I learned many lessons in school that left indelible marks on me. There were two that shook me up, and I felt condemned that I tend to judge people and not be understanding. As was my practice, I was standing at the entrance of the school to greet students and staff as they walked in. One morning, a colleague of mine walked past me without a greeting. I made a point of greeting her—it was not in kindness, but to teach her a lesson! She returned my greeting and went on to her class. I was still ruminating on this and felt rebuked but reasoned that she should not ignore children who will be learning from a teacher's awareness of them! After the morning assembly, this teacher walked into my office, apologized, and told me the reason. She had a difficult husband, and that morning he had created a scene, and she had left her diamond earrings on the dresser and was concerned that the maid who works in her home would take them! I apologized to her and struggled with myself for my wrong assessment.

At the time of the annual school fete, several mothers volunteered to sew dresses for girls. Sometimes we gave them material and patterns and skeins. One mother was a good seamstress and made lovely dresses for her girls. She volunteered to sew dresses, and we were disappointed. When the mother came to see me, the first thing she did was to apologize to me. She showed me her arthritic fingers and added, "These are not good for the stall. I came to tell you that I will buy them for the price you fix." I refused to let her buy them and thanked her and felt wretched that I did not have compassion to understand the problems of people. I pray always that I will have a loving heart and not come to hasty and wrong conclusions.

If God looks "beyond my faults and sees my need," who am I, with many faults, to judge others? I get emotional when I hear Dottie Rambo's hymn sung to the tune of the Irish folksong "Danny Boy." God's love is amazing.

Appendix

The Family History
Written by Havajee Atreya Rao

out line of our family History.
The Savajees of Nasik & Tanjore.

Maharastra is bounded on the North along the southern edge of the Satpura Mountains, up to the point where the river Wainganga bends south to join the Godavery. From that point the boundary turns S. West by an irregular line till it reaches Goa on the Arabian Sea. This sea is the western boundary up to a little south of Surat on the Tapti river. The coastal strip is called The Konkan and the people, the Konkanese. The Konkani Brahmins eat fish and so there were no inter marriages between them and the other Mahratta Brahmins. The Konkani Brahmins are also called Saraswati Brahmins or Chitpawans. The Peshwas were Chitpawans.

In the North, the highlands of the Central Indian Plateau containing Nasik in the north, Poona in the West and Kolhapur in the south, was called Kandesh. (Konadesh or triangular country) and the mahrattas highlanders are called Deshasthas.

Those living south of Kandesh are called Dakshine or Kannada Maharashtra of the Maratha. The language is mixed with Kanarese. As the dress, habits and customs of the Kanarese & Maharattas are almost same, there is a mixture in language and blood also between the two peoples in this area. Miraj, Sangli, Gadag, Hubli & Dharwar, are in this part of Maharashtra. There were free inter marriages between the Deshasthas and the Southern Maharattas, as well as the Kanarese.

As far back as I know, our ancestor was Balaji Rao Savajee, a Deshastha Brahmin of Atreyasa Gotra, a brilliant scholar whose Reforms in the Mahratta language was well known. He was a contemporary of Shahjahan and was the family priest and hence Dewan of Maloji Bhonsle and Shahji Bhonsle, the grandfather and father respectively of Shivaji Bhonsle. They belonged to Nasik.

To a Muslim Mahratta, a priest is a born enemy. The hatred was like that between Hannibal & Rome, or between Israel and

Edom of old or the Arabs at present.

Ahmednagar ruled over Kandesh and were enemies to Delhi Mughals. Perhaps more due to hatred of the Mughals than love for the Sultanet of Ahmednagar, Shahji Bhonsle took service in the Ahmednagar army & was a general. He was given Poona as a jagir. Shahji fought the Mughals, who had already annexed Godavar & Berar Sultanets and had been attacking Ahmednagar from the time of Chand Bibi & Ahmednagar joined hands with the rebellious Mughal Viceroy (Subhdar) of Deccan, General Khan Jahan Lodi. Shahji harassed the Mughals. Khan Jahan Lodi was defeated & killed in 1632. Ahmednagar itself was defeated and annexed in 1637.

Shahji took service under the Sultan of Bijapur and got Bangalore jagir. Balaji Rao's family stuck to Shahji & were given properties in Bangalore, most of which was sold off by my father's maternal uncle. (My father's sister was married into the Arni Rajah's family & was given jewelry worth about Rs. 50,000·00 while she came to her father's house they were stolen. To replace them of the same weight & pattern, most of the Bangalore properties were sold by their uncle, my father's father Narayan Rao Havaji having died when my father was only 2 years old.

Shahji had three sons 1) Sambhaji (senior) was killed in a battle, 2) Shivaji & 3) Venkoji. Shivaji did not compromise with any Moslems refused to join Bijapur army. When presented at Court, he did not follow the Muslim custom of offering Tasleem, but gave a namaskar with head erect. The Sultan pretended not to notice, but Shahji sent him off to Poona, with his mother Jeeji Bai & tutor Dadaji. It handed down from his 19th year Shivaji's raiding activities began. His raids into Bijapur territories brought Shahji into dis-favour. Shahji retired to his Bangalore jagir, was brought to Bijapur, imprisoned & on Shahjahans intervention released. Shivaji carved out a kingdom first, from Goa to Kalyan, in Konkan & he chose a Chitpavan as his

Dewan or Peshwa, while Havajees continued with
Venkoji at Bangalore.

The Naik ruler of Trichinopoly sought the
hand of the princess of Tanjore but this was refused
by Tanjore Rajah. Thereupon, the Naik induced
the Mahrattas at Bangalore to attack Tanjore.
When they attacked Tanjore Fort, the Rajah lost all
hopes of successful defence and put his daughter
in a room surrounded by sacks of gunpowder &
as the Mahrattas burst into the fort, he blew up his
daughter into eternity.

Tanjore became a Maharatta Kingdom under
Bhonsle rulers and Havajees obtained as inams
rich lands in Mayavaram & Kannargudi. My
fathers ancestral home in Mayavaram was at
the beginning of PATTAMANGALAM street, where
a stream called PALAYA (old) Kaveri flowed by
their backyard.

My grandfather was Narayan Rao, who died
when my father was only 2 years old. He had an
elder son Hari Rao & three daughters. The Havaja
line always continued precariously through one
son. If a man had more than one son, the others
either died unmarried, or childless or had only
daughters. My father's brother had one son, Krishna
Rao, who died unmarried, and three daughters. My
father's name was Hettur Sherma. When still
a baby in the cradle, a cobra was found coiled
by his side and my grandmother prayed & vowed
that, if the cobra left without harming her son,
she would give the child Adi Sesha's name. It
glided up the cradle ropes & from then my
father became Seshagiri Rao.

My father's mother was partly Kanarese
belonging to the family of Dewan Poorniah,
the Dewan of Haider Ali Khan, whose brilliant
Dewanship helped prosperity of Mysore state
I shall give you Poorniah's history another
time.

Descending from Balaji Rao and more recently

From Ponniah, my father's family inherited abilities above average. My grand-father & after him my father's brother, inherited the position of spiritual heads of the Maharatta's in the South. My father could talk, read & write 8 languages, Mahratti, Sanskrit, Tamil, Telugu, Kanarese, Malayalam, Arabic & English. As he began to learn English after Marati, Sanskrit & Tamil, my uncle forbade it, saying that his English would lead him to accept their religion. As tho' my father persisted in his studies of English, my uncle tied him to a post & ~~lashed too~~ thrashed him with a coir rope. On release, my father left home for Bangalore where a maternal uncle of his, Raja Sir T. Madhava Rao, was Dewan of Mysore. As a maternal uncle, he was a guardian to my father & my uncle could not take him back. Sir Madhava Rao's son Prasada Rao, who later became a Dewan of Mysore, was himself studying English so my father could continue his English studies.

My uncles fear about my father accepting the religion of the English, suggested to him that, their religion could not be bad as they had defeated the Maharattas & ruled the country. My mother's father's family had already become Christians & so my father contacted my maternal grand father & studied the Holy Bible. In the meanwhile my father's brother died & my father had to become the spiritual head. His mother came to Bangalore & found him studying the Bible & she raised hell with my grand-father, who gave the Bible & taught my father how to pray & seek God's guidance

My father followed the advice, the Holy Bible & the Holy Spirit, guided him. It was good, as he was not bound down by creeds & dogmas, and till his death, lived a prayerful, enlightened & righteous life, with love from God & His creation, including all living creatures.

My father joined the Railways but being shocked by witnessing a fatal accident to two of his staff, he left the service & joined the P.& T. dept. He did not ask for Baptism till his mother died and he had performed the first annual death ceremony (Samvathsirakam). He was threatened with death if he became a Christian & not a muslim, by a Moplah zamindar at Badagara. He wired to Calicut for protection, while a Moplah mob lay waiting for him in a Mango tope opposite. He got police help & was transferred to Calicut. There he contacted the Basle mission & they told him that in their mission women should not wear ornaments like the Penticostals of today. So he took Baptism from in the C.M.S. His Baptismal certificate was signed by Bishop Gell of Calicut.

He abandoned his ancestral property as it was stained with the blood of a pure, innocent princess. He made your father & me to promise to claim it or even accept it, even if it were offered to us. Even in Gunner's street, before his death, he made us promise him the same again.

After your father, I am the only descendant in my generation, of Balaji Rao Havajee, But thank God, I have 7 sons, 3 of whom, Prasad (Pedda) Sanli (Bhasker) & Gunni (Jeswant) have already one little Havajee each, I hope there will be enough Havajees at the Lord's second coming, thanks to my father's secession & my mother's father's evangelism.

uncle

Outline of Our Family History[1]

By Havajee Atreya Rao

The Havajees of Nasik & Tanjore

Maharashtra is founded on the North along the southern edge of the Satpura Mountains, up to the point where the Wainganga bends south to join the Godavari. From that point the boundary turns S.West, by an irrigation line till it reaches Goa on the Arabian Sea. This sea is the western boundary up to a little south of Surat on the Tapti river. The coastal strip is called the Konkan and the people, the Konkenese. The Konkani Brahmins eat fish and so there were no inter-marriages between them and the other Maharashtra Brahmins. The Konkani Brahmins are also called Saraswathi Brahmins or Chitpavans. The Peshwas were Chitpavans.

In the North, the highlands of the Central Indian Plateau containing Nasik on the north, Poone in the west and Kolhapuri in the south was called Kandesh (Konadesh or Triangular Country) and the Maharatta highlanders are called Deshasthas.

Those living south of Kandesh are called Dakshina or Kannada Maharattas. The language is mixed with Kanarese as the dress, habits and the customs of the Kanarese & Maharattas are almost same. There is a mixture in language and blood between the two peoples in the area. Maraj, Sangli, Gadag, Hubli & Dharwan, are in this part of Maharashtra. There were free inter-marriages between the Deshasthas and the southern Maharattas, as well as the Kanarese.

As far as I know, our ancestor was Balaji Rao Havajee, a Deshastha Brahmin of Atreyasa Gotra, a brilliant scholar whose reform in the Maharatta Language was well known. He was a contemporary of Shahjahan and was the family priest and Levee Dewan of Maloji Bhoisle and Shalji Bhoisle, the grandfather and father, respectively, of Shivaji Bhoisle. They belonged to Nasik.

To a Mahratta, a Muslim is a born enemy. The hatred was like that between Hannibal & Rome or between Israel and Edom of old or the Arabs at present. Ahmednagar ruled over Kandesh and were enemies to Delhi Mughals. Perhaps more due to hatred of the Mughals than love for the Sultanas of Ahmednagar, Shivaji Bhoisle took service in the Ahmednagar army & was a general. He was given Poone as a Jagir. Shivaji fought the Mughals, who had already annexed Bidar & Berar Sultanater and had been attacking Ahmednagar from the time of Chand Bili & Ahmednagar joined hands with the rebellious Mughal Viceroy (Subiddar) of Deccan, General Khan Jahan Loidi. Shivaji harassed the Moghuls. Khan Jahan Loidi was defeated & killed in 1632. Ahmednagar itself was defeated and annexed in 1637.

Shaliji took service under the Sultan of Bijapur and got Bangalore Jagir. Balaji Rao's family stuck to Shivaji & were given properties in Bangalore, most of which was sold off by my father's maternal uncle. My father's sister was married into the Arni Rajha's family & was given jewelry worth about Rs. 50,000.00. When she came to her father's house they were stolen. To replace them of the same weight & pattern, most of the Bangalore properties were sold by their uncle, my father's father Narayana Rao Havajee having died when my father was only 2 years old.

Shaliji had three sons: 1) Sambhaji (senior) was killed in a battle, 2) Shivaji 9, 3) Venkoji. Shivaji did not compromise with any Moslem & refused to join Bijapur army. When presented at court, he did not follow the Moslem custom of offering Tasleem, but gave a namaskar with head erect. The Sultan pretended not to notice, but Shaliji sent him off to Poone with his mother Jeaji Bai & tutor Dadaji Khandesh. From his 19th year Shivaji's raiding activities began. His raids into Bijapur territories brought Shahji into disfavor. Shahji retired to his Bangalore jagir, was brought to Bijapur, imprisoned & on Shahjahan's intervention released. Shivaji carved out a kingdom first, from Goa to Kalyan, in Konkan & he appointed a Chitpavan as his Dewan or Peshwa, while Havajees continued with Venkoji at Bangalore.

The Naik ruler of Trichinopoly sought the hand of the princess of Tanjore but this was refused by Tanjore Rajah. Thereupon, the Naik induced the Mahrattas at Bangalore to attack Tanjore. When they attacked Tanjore Fort, the Rajah lost all hopes of successful defense and put his daughter in a room surrounded by sacks of gunpowder as the Mahrattas burst into the Fort, he blew up his daughter into eternity.

Tanjore became a Mahratta Kingdom under Bhoisle rulers and Havajees obtained as inams rich lands in Mayavaram & Mannargudi. My father's ancestral home in Mayavaram was at the beginning of Pattamangalam street where a stream called Palaya (old) Kaveri flowed by their backyard.

My grandfather was Narayan Rao, who died when my father was only 2 years old. He had an elder son Hari Rao & three daughters. The Havajee line always continued precariously through one son. If a man had more than one son, the others either died unmarried or childless or had only daughters. My father's brother had only one son, Krishna Rao, who died unmarried, and three daughters. My father's name was Hethu Sherma. When still a baby in the cradle, a Cobra was found coiled by his side and my grandmother prayed & vowed that, if the Cobra left without harming her son, she would give the child Adi Sesha's name. It glided up the cradle ropes & from then my father became Seshagiri Rao.

My father's mother was partly Kanarese belonging to the family of Dewan Poorniah, the Dewan of Haidar Ali khan, whose brilliant Dewanship helped prosperity of Mysore state. I should give you Poormiah's history another time.

Descending from Balaji Rao and more recently from Poorniah, my father's family inherited abilities above average. My grandfather & after him my father's brother, inherited the position of spiritual heads of the Mahrattas in the south. My father could talk, read and write 8 languages- Mahratti, Sanskrit, Tamil, Telugu, Kannarese, Malayalam, Arabic & English. As he began to learn English after Mahratti, Sanskrit and Tamil, my uncle forbade it, saying that his English would lead him to accept their religion. As my father persisted in his studies of English, my uncle tied him to a post & thrashed him with a coir rope. On release my father left for Bangalore where a maternal uncle of his, Raja Sir T. Madhava Rao, was Dewan of Mysore. As a maternal uncle he was a guardian to my father & my uncle could not take him back. Sir Madhava Rao's son, Prasada Rao, who later became a Dewan of Mysore, was himself studying English & so my father could continue his English studies.

My uncle's fear about my father accepting the religion of the English, suggested to him that, their religion could not be bad as they had defeated the Maharashtra & ruled the country. My mother's father's family had already become Christians & so my father contacted my maternal grandfather and studied the Holy Bible. In the meanwhile, my father's brother died & my father had to become the spiritual head. His mother came to Bangalore and found him studying the Bible. She raised hell with my grandfather, who gave the Bible & taught my father how to pray and seek God's guidance. My father followed the advice. The Holy Bible and the Holy Spirit guided him. It was good, as he was not bound down by creeds & dogmas, and till his death, lived a prayerful, enlightened & righteous life, with love for God & His creation, including all living creatures.

My father joined the Railways but being shocked by witnessing a fatal accident of two of his staff, he left the service & joined the P&T dept. He did not ask for baptism till his mother died and he had performed the first annual death ceremony (Samvathsirikam). He was threatened with death if he became a Christian & not a Muslim by a Moplah Zamindar at Badagara. He wired to Calicut for protection, while a Moplah mob lay waiting for him in Mango *tope* opposite. He got police help & was transferred to Calicut. There he contacted the Basle [Basel] Mission & they told him that in their mission women should not wear ornaments like the Pentecostals of today. So he took baptism in the E.M.S. His baptismal certificate was signed by Bishop Jell of Calicut.

He abandoned his ancestral property as it was stained with the blood of a pure, innocent princess. He made your father & me, to promise never to claim it or even accept it, even if it were offered to us. Even in Gunner's street, before his death, he made us promise him the same again.

After your father, I am the only descendant in my generation, of Balaji Rao Havajee. But thank God, I have 7 sons, 3 of whom, Prasad (Pedda), Santi (Bhaskar) & Gunni (Jeswanth) have already one little Havajee each, I hope there will be enough Havajees at the Lord's second coming. Thanks to my father's decision & my mother's father's evangelism.

Uncle
Havajee Atreya Rao

Note

[1] The author received this letter from her uncle, her father's younger brother. The original wording of the letter has been preserved.

CPSIA information can be obtained
at www.ICGtesting.com
Printed in the USA
LVHW081530240721
693510LV00042B/1404